Jackie Huba / Ben McConnell

CREATING CUSTOMER EVANGELISTS

How Loyal Customers Become a Volunteer Sales Force

Revised Edition

LEWIS LANE PRESS

©2012 by Jackie Huba and Ben McConnell

Published by Lewis Lane Press
Austin, Texas

Printed in the United States of America

ISBN-13: 978-0-9881954-0-0

The Library of Congress has cataloged the hardcover edition as follows:

McConnell, Ben.
    Creating customer evangelists : how loyal customers become a volunteer sales force /
Ben McConnell, Jackie Huba.
        p. cm.
    Includes bibliographical references and index.
    ISBN 0-7931-5561-4
    1. Customer relations. 2. Relationship marketing. I. Huba, Jackie. II. Title.
HF5415.5.M1834 2002
658.8—dc21

For our parents—Matt and Betty, John and Kass

CONTENTS

After we launched the Macintosh in 1984, hundreds of Macintosh user groups sprang up around the world. They were gatherings of passionate believers who helped each other become better Mac users. They sustained Macintosh when Apple couldn't—or wouldn't.

Don't get me wrong: We didn't know what we were doing. This stuff was just happening, and we did our best to keep "it" happening, where "it" = "Create unbelievably loyal customers and ignite a holy war between operating platforms."

After this experience, I wrote *Selling the Dream* to evangelize evangelism. But that was 1989, and it was a different marketing world. We didn't have the Internet, 500 channels of cable TV, satellite radio, or cell phone spam.

Now the entire world is drenched and debauched in content and advertising, and we need evangelism even more. We sure don't need more stinkin' ads. We need more folks who spread the good news. This customer religion is built on great products and services. The next step is fueling the fire of customer love, and this is what this book explains.

There are four reasons why the evangelistic customer approach is important: (Some readers will know that I usually deliver such pronouncements in a top ten format, but considering that this is a foreword and space is limited, I'll keep it short.)

1. It's cheap. You don't need to pay evangelists. Most of the time, you just need to get out of their way.

2. It's effective. Think about the last significant purchase that you made: What was the biggest influence? Probably the word-of-mouth reputation of the product, not a Super Bowl commercial.

3. It's fun. How much better can it get than working with people who love your product or service and want to help make the world a better place?

4. It will drive your competition crazy when they see hundreds or thousands of customers turn into raging thunderlizards for your products and services.

Those are some of the key lessons you'll learn from *Creating Customer Evangelists.* I wish I had written this book, but I'm glad that I didn't have to, because writing a good foreword is a lot easier than writing a great book.

Guy Kawasaki
CEO
Garage Technology Ventures
Palo Alto, California

ACKNOWLEDGMENTS

It takes a community.

Writing a book requires a tremendous level of collaboration from multiple sources, some of which are named in the chapters of this book. Others played behind-the-scenes, yet vital, roles.

We are very grateful for the assistance of the leaders of our case story companies and their teams. They devoted many hours of what probably seemed an endless array of interviews, e-mails, phone calls, and fact checking. We are thankful to:

Maxine Clark, Teresa Kroll, and Katy Hartrich of Build-A-Bear Workshop.

Mark Cuban, Matt Fitzgerald, George Killebrew, and George Prokos of the Dallas Mavericks.

Tim O'Reilly, Mark Brokering, Catherine Brennan, Sara Winge, and Sandy Torre of O'Reilly & Associates.

Gerald Haman of SolutionPeople.

Jim Parker, Kevin Krone, Linda Rutherford, and Patty Kryscha of Southwest Airlines.

The following people took the time to talk with us about many concepts in the book: Richard Alm, Jeffrey "Hemos" Bates, Chris Bontrager, Jeanne Cusick, Brian Erwin, Melissa Giovagnoli, Alex Johnston, Guy Kawasaki, Evelyn McClure, Ann McGee-Cooper, Rich Marcotte, Karen Mishra, Kevin Olsen, Emanuel Rosen, Heath Row, Liz Ryan, Tim Sanders, Jackie Sloane, Daryl Urquhart, and Todd Walley.

We are extremely thankful to a stalwart group of friends and colleagues who reviewed our manuscript and made it more readable. Our thanks go to Lynn Barney, Nancy Cobb, Kevin Dowling, Betsy Harman, Kass Huba, John Huba, Dan Limbach, Matthew Lindenburg, Betty McConnell, Matthew McConnell, Lynne Marie Parson, and Simone Paddock. Their thoughts, ideas, and suggestions helped us tremendously; any errors or omissions rest solely with the authors. We'd also like to thank Victoria Rock and Tara Bonaventura of Victoria's Transcription Service for their timely help. Mary B. Good, Leslie Banks, and Elizabeth Bacher were extremely supportive as we prepared the hardcover edition.

Even though this section is becoming about as long as an Academy Awards speech, we want to publicly thank several other gracious friends who helped us and have evangelized our work to the world: Donna Itzoe, Greg Heaps, Liza Ewell, Lee Mann, Simone Paddock, Richard Landman, Todd Hassell, Tonja Rizai, Kathleen Peterson, Betsy Harman, and Melissa Giovagnoli. We also thank the accommodating staff of Starbucks Coffee at North Avenue and Wells in Chicago, where we spent several hundred hours writing and editing this work.

We'd like to acknowledge two women who, over the last year, showed us what the power of evangelism is all about: Lynne Marie Parson and Stacey Wagoner. Thanks for your enthusiasm and support. Thanks to authors Emanuel Rosen and Dan Pink for their wisdom and guidance, and to Guy Kawasaki for being an inspiration.

CHAPTER ONE

A Customer Evangelism Manifesto

We are encouraging our clients to fly Southwest Airlines. We are buying more stock . . . and we stand ready to do anything else to help. Count on our continuing support.[1]

—Southwest Airlines customer **Ann McGee-Cooper,** in an October 2001 letter to the company

You are an evangelist.

You tell others what movie to see, which computer to purchase, what restaurant to visit, which dentist you prefer, which cell phone to buy, which books to read, which clubs to join. Your recommendations are sincere. Passionate, perhaps. Perhaps you didn't realize that you are an evangelist—a bringer of glad tidings—but your sphere of influence, made up of friends, family, colleagues, and professional communities, realizes it. You may be the go-to person for all manner of recommendations.

Ann McGee-Cooper is an evangelist for Southwest Airlines. After the 9/11 attacks, which crippled and jeopardized airlines for months, McGee-Cooper wrote Southwest a letter. In it, she said she was persuading clients, friends, and family members to fly Southwest. She was purchasing tickets on their behalf. She bought the company's stock. Perhaps most tellingly, she included a $500 check with her letter, saying that the airline needed the money "more than I do."[2] She is more than a loyal customer; she is a customer evangelist.

She stood by a company she loves and offered her help. With apologies to airlines, that's a significant accomplishment. Airlines often consider loyal customers as those who accumulate the most frequent flyer miles. This is true for other businesses, too, such as grocery stores, clothing stores, pipe-making companies, or furniture manufacturers; they may define loyal customers as those who purchase repeatedly. But that style of loyalty is often driven by convenience or low prices. Very often, their customers are repeat customers, not necessarily loyal customers.

Relying on frequent-purchasers exclusively as a model of loyalty is a faulty system. A frequent purchaser may purchase from you but not recommend you. He may even bad-mouth you to friends, colleagues, or customers in line or online for a number of reasons. But a customer evangelist not only purchases from you regularly, she feels compelled to spread the word. Ann McGee-Cooper considers Southwest part of her family, and she would never publicly bad-mouth a family member. This doesn't mean that Southwest is for everyone; it has its share of detractors who don't care for its policies of no reserved seats and low frills. But your business isn't for everyone, either.

What makes Southwest and other companies with dedicated armies of evangelists stand apart from their competitors? They have crossed the emotional chasm that separates most businesses with customers. They have made or facilitated a connection. Therefore, their customers *believe*. They believe enough that they will assuredly recommend you. They will put their personal reputation on the line on your behalf. Companies like Southwest create evangelistic loyalty not through a paid referral system, or by having the lowest prices (nearly all of the airlines are economically competitive), or by creating the fanciest Web site (Southwest's is quite utilitarian, but not beautiful). They do it by being authentic. Southwest's executives boil it down to "doing business by the Golden Rule." They hire empathetic people. They encourage their employees to have fun on the job. They want their employees to talk like real people. It's the opposite of what most business executives consider a professional "corporate" relationship with customers, which often turns employees into corporate robots, the most inauthentic type of employee possible. Most people do not talk like an ad, or a press release, or a company spokeswoman quoted in the paper. When you screw up and miss your kid's soccer game, you don't say, "We acknowledge the pain and suffering incurred by the parties herein, but we do not admit wrongdoing. We wish Mr. Smith Jr. the best in his future endeavors."

When we set out to understand what created evangelists for our case-study companies, we discovered a simple yet undeniable truth: *People are loyal to people, not necessarily brands.* That's the magic bullet about word of mouth and how it spurs evangelism. People are loyal to people, not necessarily brands. There are a number of ways to create and build word of mouth on the pathway to loyalty and customer evangelism, and that's what this book is about. We'll introduce you to the people behind the scenes at Southwest and how they have defied all odds to become the most successful airline company in history. We'll introduce you to Maxine Clark, the visionary retailer of Build-A-Bear Workshop who started with a great idea for one store and turned it into a chain earning hundreds of millions of dollars in less than seven years. You'll meet Mark Cuban, the plucky and outspoken owner of the Dallas Mavericks and an entreprenerial billionaire who loves to hang out with fans. We'll introduce you to Tim O'Reilly, whose company has become one of the vanguards of technology leadership, primarily because of Tim's vision and connections with other technology leaders. You'll meet Gerald Haman, who has focused his career on innovating the innovation process. His process involves karaoke and dressing up in costumes. Not exactly the academic approach to innovation, which is why he's built an evangelistic roster of client companies. And you'll learn how the starched-shirt company of all companies, IBM, loosened up, gave up control, and built an evangelistic following by supporting a software revolution rather than fighting it.

Before we get into the principal ways of how to create customer evangelists, it's important to understand what they are and how they behave, as well as the differences between repeat purchasers and the true believers. It may turn out that for your business, you already have evangelists. Here are seven clues:

1. They passionately recommend your company to friends, neighbors, and colleagues. *Passionate* is the keyword. A nice-to-have product or service does not inspire evangelism. A must-have product does. New customers are made because a friend wouldn't stop talking about a product or service, especially how it changed her life.

2. They believe in the company and its people. People are loyal to people, not necessarily to brands. Belief in a company comes from customers or employees simply professing their trust in your people. That may rise to a higher level, too: Customers may actually profess their belief in your mission statement, especially if it is focused on changing the world.

3. They purchase your products and services as gifts. What better icon to trust and belief in your company than when a customer buys your product not once or twice, but multiple times?

4. They provide unsolicited praise or suggestions of improvement. They have moved beyond simple word of mouth into deep-rooted evangelism by offering you their time and knowledge. They have pressed themselves into volunteerism.

5. They forgive occasional subpar seasons or dips in customer service. Because they have invested some time in understanding your business, they know the score. They understand the challenges of running a business and that no one is perfect. Since they have crossed the emotional chasm with you, they have a relationship with you, and relationships are never perfect.

6. They do not want to be bought; they extol your virtues freely. To create a paid-referral system is to monetize a relationship, like paying a family member to show up for dinner. It's possible, but it forever changes the dynamic of the relationship. Paying customer evangelists turns volunteerism into labor.

7. They feel part of something bigger than themselves. They have connected with your brand or company at an intrinsic, emotional level. If your company inspires customers to meet one another and join the revolution you are inspiring—creating a community—customers feel connected to something that gives them meaning. Call it silly, ridiculous, or impossible, but it's real. The question becomes, are you ready to accept it?

The lessons from the original evangelists—the religious believers who roamed the back ways of the world to spread the word of their faith—teach us that beliefs are based on emotional connection, deep-seated convictions, and the promise of a better way. Strongly held beliefs compel many of us to tell others. The root of the word "evangelist" is based on "a bringer of the glad tidings." But this book is not about religion. It's an argument that traditional marketing practices have ceased to enjoy their dominance and are being usurped by word of mouth and customer-driven referrals as the valuable new currency in an organization's growth.

The marketing world has changed dramatically since the advent of the 21st century. Technology has leveled the playing field to make quality less of a competitive advantage. With globalization, product and service levels have nearly evened out, as have price advantages. We're drowning in a sea of media and information overload. In a world with so much choice, how do people make decisions? By relying on trusted friends, colleagues, or family members. In the new world of marketing, evangelists act as key influencers on future customers. The ideal scenario is when a customer has been made on your behalf well before they hand over their credit card.

Not long after *Creating Customer Evangelists* was first published, *Harvard Business Review* published the results of research conducted by Fred Reichheld. He found empirical evidence correlating year-to-year revenue growth with the number of people who recommended a company or brand. The more people who recommend a product or service, the better its chances of growing. Instead of calling them evangelists, Reichheld termed them "net promoters": the sum total of people who recommend a brand, product, or company after the total number of people who don't recommend it (or are undecided) are subtracted. The resulting sum provides what he calls the "net promoter score."[3] With the help of a research firm that gathers customer surveys, he studied three industries, including airlines, and what happened with their businesses between 1999 and 2002. The research firm examined tens of thousands of customer surveys from the period, which happened to include a "would you recommend X company" question. After analyzing the surveys, they found strong year-over-year correlations between the total net promoter scores of individual airlines and their annual revenue growth. The airline that had the highest recommendability score? Southwest. It was dramatically out front, far ahead of its competitors in recommendability. It also had the best revenue growth of all airlines during the period. TWA was the worst-rated company; it eventually went out of business in 2001 when American Airlines purchased its assets.

To understand the recommendability of your product, brand, or company, discovering if customers would recommend it to friends, colleagues, or family members is a strong start toward building an analytical understanding of loyalty and evangelism.

"'Who's to blame/for this state of distress?'
'It's the Marketing Director!' we all confessed."[4]

If it's not the messenger that companies shoot first, then it's the marketing director. In 2001, Harpell, a Massachusetts ad agency, surveyed prospective technology marketing managers to discover their pains. Respondents said, "My budget's been cut but I have to produce more." "I'm on my way out the door." "My staff's been cut." It was a bleak report. As part of a marketing campaign to promote its services, Harpell produced an old-timey, saloon-style song with plunky piano about the trials and tribulations of a marketing director who is continually blamed for lackluster sales. Harpell reminds us that whether it's the marketing director's fault or not, she usually takes the bullet for disappointing sales. Why? There are a variety of reasons why traditional marketing is faltering.

Marketing today is based on 1960s principles. Most college marketing classes still teach the 4 P's: product, place, price, and promotion. E. Jerome McCarthy introduced the 4 P's in 1960, and decades later, most marketing education programs are still based on the 4 P's. That's a testament to the durability of McCarthy's scholarship, but promotion, the fourth of the four, has probably undergone the most radical change. In its original incarnation, promotion was focused on advertising, sales promotion, public relations, and personal selling. Most college marketing textbooks cover very little, if any, about word of mouth and customer evangelism. Part of the reason is that there is very little academic research into the subject. That began to change somewhat in 2005 as a few academics began to focus on word of mouth as a discipline. The Word of Mouth Marketing Association was formed in 2005, too, giving the nascent industry some form and shape.

Marketing is advertising. The next time you're at cocktail party, ask someone for their definition of marketing. Chances are they'll say its advertising. Worse yet, your imbibing test subject may define marketing as telemarketing, which is more like caveman marketing—hunt random fields of prey and beat the ones you can catch into submission. Unfortunately, the common definition of marketing is what we are bombarded with every day: advertising. Author

David Shenk surmises the average person is exposed to more than 3,000 advertising messages per day.[5] Our senses are under continual assault, much of it by bad or meaningless information. Which marketing professionals are glamorized in the media? Ad executives. Remember the devious ad agency owner played by Heather Locklear on the television show *Melrose Place*? How about the lead male characters and their ad agency on the show *Thirtysomething*? Dustin Hoffman was the beleaguered father and ad agency executive in the Oscar-winning film *Kramer vs. Kramer*. The Darrin Stevens character from the popular *Bewitched* TV sitcom was an ad man. Ad execs, all of them! When was the last time a customer service manager was the hero of a blockbuster film? Don't answer that.

Power goes to those with the biggest budgets. How do some marketing managers measure their success in the corporate hierarchy? By the size of their advertising budgets. Bigger ad budgets are often more about coalescing internal power; the bigger the budget, the more influence you wield internally and with external partners. Helping customers solve problems is not necessarily at the top of the list. At some large companies, you had better spend your annual budget completely or you'll receive less money next year. What's the fastest way to spend money? Mass advertising. Ambitious marketers are given few incentives for creating customer evangelists and word-of-mouth programs that cost dramatically less than mass media budgets. Unfortunately, many company marketers are promoted and hired based on the size of the budget they grew or managed, not always on the results they delivered, the word of mouth they inspired, or the loyalty they engendered.

Marketing must produce immediate results. Our technological society demands instant gratification. We want our food fast and our Internet connections blazing. Why save up and pay cash for something when you can have it now on credit? So it goes for marketing. The stock market rewards companies for growing revenues and profits quarter by quarter. Wall Street has no interest in long-term investment. The Street does not want to hear about money spent on customer evangelism and loyalty programs. Investment bankers are prone to care primarily about the number of new customers you will generate in the next 12 weeks. Revenues down? The Street wants to know what ad campaigns you're planning. It rewards layoffs with a stock-price bump. If sales are slipping, panicked CEOs often order marketing directors to throw more money at print materials for the field sales force. Or to create a new and more aggressive telemarketing campaign.

Marketing is desperate. The globalization of commerce has produced an economy rich with choices. How do we decide, really, between 165 cereal products and 85 different breakfast bars? Every day, we are inundated with ads on television, buses, under computer browser windows, in the waiting rooms of physicians and dentists, on phone cards, on the backs of lottery tickets, and on banners towed by noisy planes circling around crowded beaches, annoying the beachgoers who are trying to get away from it all. At 3,000 advertisement exposures per day, that's 188 messages per hour, three per minute, every minute of every day.

With so much competition, mass media ads must scream louder and more often just to squeeze through the clutter. In 1980, ad agency pioneer David Ogilvy argued that ads must run at least nine times before a future customer grasps your message. That made sense for an ad executive of his time; he made money from the size of your ad budget and the number of times you ran ads, and he happily purchased them for you with a sweet commission fee. Desperation marketing is easy to spot: please, please, please . . . nine or more times . . . buy our product! Continuous repetition is like adding water to the ocean. If a company cannot differentiate its products or focus on a specific target audience, then it usually settles for advertising "the lowest price," the last refuge of a company that has lost its way.

Marketing to new customers is sexy. Evidence shows that acquiring a new customer is five times more expensive than keeping a current customer happy. Moreover, customer profitability tends to grow the longer a customer stays with you. It costs less to keep them coming back for more. Yet we see many otherwise bright, college-educated marketers spend millions of dollars on advertising, direct mail, and the nebulous concept of "branding"—all in the name of acquiring new customers. Why? It's the thrill of the chase. The opening scene in *Kramer vs. Kramer* shows Dustin Hoffman accepting congratulations from his ad agency peers; he says that landing the coveted $2 million Revlon account was "one of the five best days of my whole life." Landing new customers is sexy, like cavemen slaying a gazelle on the grasslands. Building the loyalty of existing customers, like gathering nuts and berries and growing a garden, is hard work. Inspiring them to spread the word is harder yet.

Mass marketing is dying. Response rates for several campaign tactics continue their inevitable decline. Measures of the average Internet banner click-through range from 0.005 to 1 percent. The average direct mail response rate is 1 to 2 percent. Response rates for television and print advertising remain unclear. Measures such as "brand awareness" and "purchase intent" are vacuous at best. Traditional message platforms are so crowded they're no longer effective. Marketing principles are from a vastly different world. Exponential growth of a media-driven culture, the ubiquity of information sources, and since 1994, the advent of the World Wide Web have made mass media effectiveness inert. Continuous, mind-numbing marketing repetition is clogging the arteries of trust and attention every day.

There's evidence for the decline among traditional advertising and the rise of word of mouth for making future purchases. Not surprisingly, the restaurant industry is the most reliant upon good word of mouth. More than eight out of ten people determine their new restaurant choices based on a referral.

How people get information about . . .

	Word of mouth	Advertising
Restaurants	83%	35%
Prescription drugs	71%	21%
Hotels	63%	27%
Cars	58%	36%
Computers	40%	18%
Financial services	57%	12%

SOURCE: Roper Reports[6]

The research firm BIGresearch found that word of mouth is the most influential media on purchase decisions, among all age groups. Here's how the top ten list rounded out:

1. Word of mouth

2. TV

3. Coupons

4. Newspaper inserts

5. Read article

6. Direct mail

7. Magazines

8. In-store promotion

9. Cable TV

10. Internet advertising[7]

How do we evolve from the primordial ocean of advertising? How do we help our best customers become our best salespeople? We've found there are six common strategies among organizations that benefit from remarkable levels of customer evangelism. We call these strategies the six tenets of customer evangelism:

1. Customer plus-delta: Continuously gather customer feedback.

2. Napsterized knowledge: Make it a point to share knowledge freely.

3. Build the buzz: Expertly build word-of-mouth networks.

4. Create community: Encourage communities of customers to meet and share.

5. Make bite-size chunks: Devise specialized, smaller offerings to get customers to bite.

6. Create a cause: Focus on making the world, or an industry, better.

How do you employ these tenets? Here are a few ideas.

1. Customer plus-delta.

Understand what evangelists *love* by continuously gathering their input. Dallas Mavericks owner Mark Cuban is a feedback machine. He conducts mini-surveys with nearly every fan he meets, asking how to improve the fan experience (the "delta" in plus-delta). His e-mail address shows up on the American Airlines Arena scoreboard. Build-A-Bear Workshop, the interactive retailer where children can build their own personal stuffed animals, uses a "Cub Advisory Board" as a feedback and decision-input body. The board is made up of twenty 8–12 year olds who review new product ideas and give a paws up or down. Maxine Clark, the company's Chief Executive Bear, says that after six years in business, 99 percent of products in the store are customer ideas.[8]

2. Napsterize your knowledge.

The original Napster, the file-sharing service introduced to the world in 1999, turned the music industry's distribution system on its ear. It popularized the concept of a fast and efficient peer-to-peer network, where products, ideas, and yes, even intellectual property, could be shared easily. But it also demonstrated that all of the above could spread quickly, too. Remove the idea of sharing someone else's intellectual property from the equation and replace it with sharing your own content. With that in place, "Napsterizing" can become a powerful distribution system to spread your ideas, products, or knowledge. The more knowledge you share with the world, the more that people will tell others about it. Fans around the world devote dozens of hours weekly to their product or company Web sites and weblogs. Embrace them. Invite them to meet your back-office team. Give them plenty of statistics, photos, and anything else they need for their Web sites. For companies that primarily sell to other companies, discover routes to sharing more information among all of your trading partners so the *experience* of being a customer becomes more valuable.

3. Build the buzz.

Customer evangelists are often information junkies. They're influencers who spread the latest news through their networks. That provides them stature and authority. They'll use many mediums to spread buzz about products or companies, whether it's face-to-face with friends and family, or huge audiences via e-mail, online forums, or chat rooms. Shepherd your evangelists into a special program, where they're given a backstage pass to try new products or meet the rock stars of your company.

4. Create community.

Provide like-minded customers the chance to meet one another. PAETEC, a telecommunications company that provides services to hotels, universities, and other companies, hosts informal customer dinners around the country. Current customers and key prospects are invited for food and good company. No boring PowerPoint presentations here; just customers talking about their telecommunications challenges and how much they love PAETEC's service and support. Prospects are sold on the company by *other* customers. When customers meet one another underneath your umbrella, the value you deliver as a vendor increases exponentially.

5. Make bite-size chunks.

Even if a customer doesn't purchase, she may spread favorable word of mouth because she could try before buying. Bite-size chunks of your products and services reduce risk and sales cycles and offer up-front value. Those are three key qualities evangelists seek out.

6. Create a cause.

Companies that strive for a higher purpose—like supporting "freedom" as Harley-Davidson and Southwest Airlines do—often find that customers, vendors, suppliers, and employees naturally root for its success. A well-defined cause can change the world, no matter how big or small. Customer evangelists crave emotional connection and validation; a well-defined cause generates strong emotional attachments.

Times change, and it's time for marketing tactics that worked for past generations to evolve from a model predicated on advertising and direct mail to one based on building customer goodwill. The continuous, mind-numbing marketing repetition that clogs the arteries of our attention every day is like one of the common definitions of insanity: doing the same thing over and over again and expecting different results. Today's always-on information has turned competition in a 24-hour playing field. To compete now and in the future, focus your energies on creating a loyal following of passionate customers who support you and evangelize everyone who will listen. Fan the flames of customer love. Demonstrate that you appreciate their support in good times and bad. Give your most passionate and loyal customers meaningful, authentic reasons to work harder for you; the investment is repaid by evangelists like Ann McGee-Cooper.

CHAPTER TWO

When Customers Believe

Sales is rooted in what's good for me. Evangelism is rooted in what's good for you.[1]

—Guy Kawasaki

The popularization of evangelism in business can be traced to Guy Kawasaki and Apple Computer in the 1980s. The company hired him as a "software evangelist" in 1983, and his job was to sell the Macintosh dream to developers who would write software for the Apple computer. The dream was to increase the productivity and creativity of people using personal computers. The Macintosh was a revolutionary product for its ease of use and unique design, drawing favorable reviews from early customers. The fervor and zeal of software evangelists like Kawasaki fostered an image of a company that wanted to change the world.

We met Kawasaki at his office in Palo Alto on a typical, sunny California day. He had since left Apple and started his own company, Garage Technology Ventures, which helps incubate new technology companies. Kawasaki has a big presence. He smiles easily. He says what's on his mind. When we stepped into his office, he apologized because he was having "a bad digital day." Many of his electronic gizmos were not working properly, including one of his several Macs, and it was stressing him out. Despite the breakdown of his Mac, he said he remained a true believer to Apple, which led naturally into our discussion of his work there. First of all, he wasn't its original "evangelist."

"The job title [of evangelist] already existed at Apple when I got there, so I didn't invent the title," he says. "It was used more in the evangelistic sense of preaching, pounding on the pavement, getting the job done, taking the battle to the customer—all that stuff." Not long after he started at Apple, its executives began to more fully appreciate the effects of the devotion it was inspiring. The devotion was not planned; it was a beneficent accident.

"The secondary effects of getting people to believe, who then got more people to believe, is something that was stumbled upon. In my recollection, I was never told, 'OK, you go get XYZ to write software, and they in turn will get more customers to buy your software and to buy Macs.' We never thought it through that much. That's what happened, but that was not the plan."[2]

The company created so many accidental customer evangelists that they organized themselves into user groups. "Apple has thousands of user groups," Kawasaki says. "Those are truly the evangelists. They're not paid. They're not employees. They tell people to use Macintosh solely for the other person's benefit. That is the difference between evangelism and sales. Sales is rooted in what's good for me. Evangelism is rooted in what's good for you."[3]

Drawing on Kawasaki's appropriate distinction, it's the return of the Golden Rule. Focusing beyond the mere product or service and its sale and to what may make a customer's life more fulfilling. Getting to root needs. By accident or by design, customer evangelism is organic in nature. It's grassroots. It sprouts from the customer and begins to bloom with customers talking with one another, and spreads as customers recruit new customers on your behalf. It blooms when customers provide you with ideas for new products, product improvements, new services, store locations, or new strategies that build on relationships with existing business partners. It's not about you, it's about them. Customer evangelists often do this root-planting work, like hobbyist gardeners. It's for the love of the experience. Conversely, the evangelism of customers is free. There's no direct cost, no commissions. It's all upside. When customers deliver new customers to your doorstep, it's a gift without reciprocity.

In most businesses, the marketing group is typically responsible for activities that acquire and retain customers. Many business leaders know that marketing is more than a department; it's a philosophy and belief system for the entire organization, like a corporate religion, and the strongest believers can be the best leaders. This is a truism for creating employee evangelists as much as customer evangelists. Companies that create organizational charts, business plans, and mission statements around the customer—not around their own internal structure—are ones that tend to create sustainable, long-term value. Customer evangelism is a theology about creating products, services, or experiences *that people will talk about*. It's an ongoing design process. Inside a business thriving with customer evangelists, plans are designed to get customers talking and coming back. These companies deliver memorable experiences that compel customers to share their experience with others. Leaders who believe in customer evangelism rely on more than the four P's, or segmentation, or optimizing distribution channels, or creating better advertising, direct mail, or all of those one-way communication systems. They earn the evangelism of customers because they focus on learning everything possible about customers and interact with them more than their competitors do. They earn a product or service recommendation and focus intently on creating loyalty at the front lines of the business, not in the back office.

As we spoke with the leaders of our case-study companies (none of which are clients, nor did we have any form of financial relationship with them), we discovered a pattern: most said their approach was about "doing the right thing." Even the biggest of the big said their marketing strategy wasn't anything out of the ordinary. Not once did we encounter an emphasis on "creating shareholder value" as the rallying cause of our case-study companies. This is not to diminish the importance of shareholder value, but companies that engineer plans and tactics with shareholder value and growing their stock prices at double-digit rates as their primary belief systems will find it difficult to build an evangelism culture. A trash heap with the likes of Enron, Arthur Andersen, Global Crossing, Sunbeam, WorldCom, and a thousand misguided dot-coms is filled with companies for which profit, shareholder value, and rising stock prices were the primary rally points.

Repeatedly, we found that our case-study companies develop relationships with customers and those relationships reflect the values of the company's culture. (This is different from CRM, or customer relationship management, which tends to imply that a multimillion-dollar investment in a CRM software package creates better customer relationships.) A customer evangelism philosophy based on customer relationships is embodied in the belief system of the company founder or chief executive. Employees in our case-study companies—from Southwest's 33,000 employees to SolutionPeople's 10—believe in the company's core philosophy toward customers and practice it. To understand a company's culture, look at its chief executive: Is he a people person? Does she focus on building relationships inside and outside the company? Approachable or untouchable? Down to earth or too unreachable?

Other questions: Does the chief executive ooze ostentation with gold cufflinks and $1,800 tailored suits? Or does he seem like a neighborly guy who would happily loan you his lawnmower? If you are the chief, do you enjoy the people part of the job? If dealing with people consistently annoys you, then you're in the wrong job, because your philosophy and nonverbal language about relationships spreads to all departments beyond the marketing group. The chief executive's personality becomes the organization's personality. How a chief executive works with employees is often a reflection of how a company treats its customers, which becomes source material for word of mouth. Most people in business are committed to the customer in spirit but lack the tools and tactics to fully embrace this commitment.

With the Internet, customer evangelism is scalable. Two components of evangelism—word of mouth and buzz—have become part of popular marketing vernacular. We believe customer evangelism is the most effective form of advertising available—and it's mostly free. It works as a fundamental marketing platform for five reasons.

1. The volunteer salesperson is a trusted friend or advisor.

2. The advice is coming from an independent source, not from the manufacturer.

3. The message is usually genuine and free of hype.

4. The value of the product or service is personalized for the recipient.

5. The referrer explains the value until it's fully understood by the recipient.

For marketers or entreprenuers, or something in between, their job is to grow those naturally occurring roots. Customer evangelism cuts through the muck of advertising clutter. Friends, family, and colleagues influence behavior and decision-making more than repetitive ads or aggressive salespeople. Customer evangelists are the ideal salespeople because they know a target audience. They *are* the target audience. They can search out and find others just like themselves. They know what prospective customers do for a living, where they live, and what their buying habits are like. They know how to translate a value proposition into a context prospects will understand. Great customer evangelists follow up with a prospect and help close the sale. Some offer to drive the new customer to the store to help buy the product. Much of this is done without company intervention or prodding. If the company intervenes with points or rewards, it risks damaging the authenticity and credibility of the evangelist because of the inherent payment system.

Customer evangelism reduces the time it takes for a prospect to make a purchase decision. George Silverman outlines this concept in *Secrets of Word-of-Mouth Marketing:* Purchasing a product or service is not a single decision but a series of decisions. "If you can identify and minimize just a few of those decision bottlenecks for your customers, you can reduce their decision time by more than half, thereby multiplying the sales and market share of your product or service," he writes.[4] Customer evangelists nurture a prospect through the decision cycle to complete the purchase.

Focusing on customer evangelism creates a new segment of customers who spread the good word about your products and services. An organization with customer evangelists tends to focus its external and internal activities on this common objective. We have identified three keys to a successful program.

1. A great product or service.

What makes a product or service great? Greatness is in the eye of the customer, but here are some common themes to consider. (Note: throughout this book, we try to use the words *product* and *service* interchangeably as we do *he* and *she*.)

Using what we call the SEAMS model, here are the aspects of a great product or service:

- Satisfies a customer need, want, or desire

- Easy to use (A great product is also easy to find and purchase.)

- A good value—a subjective measure defined by the customer but ultimately is the customer's belief that the benefits of the service are worth the money

- Makes the customer's life better, improving the personal or professional condition of the purchaser

- Solves a customer problem that sometimes the customer didn't know he had

How do you know if your products and services are great? Ask your customers. Ask what they *love* about your products or services. Ask what they say when they tell others about them. Begin by looking for what they say on Internet bulletin boards and in discussion groups. Quality alone doesn't guarantee success. The landscape of business history is littered with superior, Goliath products defeated by more nimble and popular Davids. Sony's Betamax system and IBM's OS/2 operating system were high quality, state of the art, and superior compared to their competition. But JVC's VHS system and Microsoft's Windows won because of expert marketing. Some people believe that as long as the end result is high quality, people will spread the word about it. This is true—but only to a point.

2. A Maniacal Focus on Customers

Most marketers and business executives contend that they are focused on customers. We understand that the purpose of business is to satisfy customer needs, yet many of us don't walk the talk. Do you? Take the following quiz.

Have you visited with a customer in the past
30 days?   Yes   No

Do you gather some form of customer input every
month?   Yes   No

Can you describe your ideal customer (not a
demographic)?   Yes   No

Do you have a customer satisfaction program?	Yes	No
Is employee compensation tied directly to customer ratings?	Yes	No
Do you know your average customer's lifetime value?	Yes	No
Does your company focus on creating memorable experiences?	Yes	No
Do your customers feel they are part of your extended family?	Yes	No
Are employees empowered to always do the right thing?	Yes	No
Are customers, suppliers, and employees treated honestly and fairly?	Yes	No

How did you score?

8–10: Congratulations; you are on your way to creating customer evangelists.

4–7: You have the right steps but not the rhythm. It will take some work.

0–4: It's time to get customer religion or wallow in obscurity.

(The appendix in this book will assist you in putting these ideas into action.)

3. Understanding That Business Is about People

In the halcyon days of the Internet bubble, the focus was on IPOs (initial public offerings), valuations, stock options, and getting big fast. In the recession that followed the bursting of the Internet bubble in early 2001, businesses slashed costs and focused on improved operational efficiency. Management by spreadsheet took over. The

I-told-you-so's said it was time to "return to basics"; *Business 2.0* aptly termed it "The Return of the Crappy Job."[5]

As Tim Sanders, author of *Love Is the Killer App,* says, "The next big thing is people."[6] Sanders implores "bizpeople" to share their knowledge, networks, and compassion. He's right. Treat your customers like your best friends; best friends support you through good times and bad. Marketers focused on people and relationships dismiss the *Art of War* as a pretense for business and embrace *The Loyalty Effect.* Successful companies "date" their customers. They ask permission to build a relationship with future customers instead of segmenting them into soulless demographic groups with campaigns to capture them like those gazelles on the grasslands.

Here's how one company dates future customers. FranklinCovey, a personal and organizational effectiveness firm located in Salt Lake City, Utah, offers a series of valuable e-mail newsletters, written by several of its senior partners, called *Helping Clients Succeed.* Free to subscribers, the newsletters offer salespeople detailed tips on developing relationships that ultimately result in sales. FranklinCovey gets instant feedback from readers on each newsletter by including a "Rate this" button in every e-mail. By requesting people to provide their e-mail address in exchange for useful information, the company has really asked permission to make its prospective customers aware of its fee-based seminars and training classes.

FranklinCovey's strategy of building relationships, by offering value up front, positions it well for creating customer evangelists. FranklinCovey vice president Mahan Khalsa is highly visible in his e-mails. We have gotten to know his warm and witty voice, literally and figuratively. His picture accompanies every e-mail, and we recognize his face with its distinctively long gray beard. Because it seems we have gotten to know him personally, he seems real and trustworthy. He is reducing the number of decisions we must make because of our growing virtual relationship with him. FranklinCovey gives away some of its knowledge, creating instant value which enables people to spread it or evangelize it.

Marketers often refer to "increasing brand loyalty" as a factor in increasing sales. But what does this terminology mean? The idea that people are loyal to brands may make some sense for consumer products that are challenging to differentiate, such as Evian versus Pellegrino. But, in general, people are loyal to people. Any business in which human beings are involved in selling or delivering a product or service has the ability to significantly influence customer experiences, thereby fostering loyalty.

Phone companies consistently score some of the lowest marks for customer service. Their monthly bills are often overly complicated and undecipherable. Some force customers to navigate a dozen voice menus before reaching a live person. Some make customers hang up and dial another number just to talk to another department. When a phone company cannot easily transfer its customers from one unit to another, it's clear that thoughtfulness about the customer experience is not a priority. When you think of your favorite restaurant, you probably remember the pleasant waitstaff or the impersonal or benignly rude host as much as, if not more than, the food. You may love the location of your apartment or office building, but the responsiveness of the landlord and/or maintenance crew influences your decision to renew or cancel your lease as much as the monthly rent. Customer evangelism is based on loyalty to people, not things.

Most traditional marketing tactics continue to decline in effectiveness but still command the majority of marketing budgets. In 2001, Pepsi hired teen pop star Britney Spears to launch a multimillion-dollar advertising campaign, one of the most expensive in the company's history. One year later, Pepsi sales were down 1 percent, a significant percentage in an industry where market share is measured in decimal points.[7] Leaders of small companies network like crazy, collect hundreds of business cards, and launch attacks of spamlike direct mail, e-mails, and phone solicitations. This approach creates a few leads and a questionable reputation. These are bad marketing habits and will never create customer evangelists.

To move toward the customer evangelism mindset, it's important to free yourself from the bonds of traditional promotion. A sizeable industry has been created to support the need to promote businesses, but most of it is oriented to talking *at* people. Advertising on TV, print, and radio; blast-faxing press releases; and a blizzard of direct mail are all one-way communications. With customer evangelism, it's important to consider promotion as a two-way process. Seth Godin's *Permission Marketing* details an approach to the back-and-forth dialogue with prospective customers that Godin likens to dating. Most people can't convince strangers in a bar to marry them; the same is true with ads that ask you to buy now. Instead, the incentive is to participate in a conversation. Over time, a customer learns about your product or service and enjoys the budding relationship. The key is conversation, not promotion. A sure sign of a bad date is when one person spends most of the date doing all the talking.

When people are loyal to people, free is easier. Pretend you have no marketing budget. (Maybe you don't have to pretend.) Word of mouth and evangelism are gifts that customers give you, but you must first earn them, for money doesn't buy goodwill. The easy way out in marketing is spending money on "branding" ads and direct mail. Instead, work harder to understand what customers love and thereby earn their admiration. It's long-term public relations, and a top-notch PR firm can be expensive. Fred Reichheld's *The Loyalty Effect* explains why companies should focus on long-term loyalty: 15 percent lower operating costs than those of comparable companies and growth rates that are 220 percent above average. Quarterly sales quotas are important but not when they drive companies to take a short-term view of taking care of customers. Focus on creating loyal customers; they are your evangelism candidates and customer evangelists will support you in the long run, in good times and bad.

Believe in your customers. If you are the analytical type, customer evangelism may seem a bit idealistic. We concede there is an ideology to the idea, but we implore organizations to back up their customer evangelism work with data. There are a few ways to consider this. First, let's consider the traditional marketing model. A marketing campaign to capture new customers costs $75,000, which sends 100,000 direct mail pieces to a rented list, resulting in 250 warm leads, which results in ten new customers who spend $20,000, returning $200,000 of new revenue. It's easy to calculate that return on investment. But how do we calculate the indifference, and perhaps the ire, of 90,000 people whom you have just spammed? How do you calculate the cost of a vigilante prospect who brandishes your direct mail piece as a stellar example of wasteful paper usage?

Marketers or entrepreneurs who spend their budgets seeking permission to develop relationships with customers will find that their investment, over time, will result in higher profits and lower operating costs. In addition to creating a noteworthy product or service, they are also focusing on building relationships. Companies that choose Wall Street as their dance partner often leave customers on the sidelines. Wall Street bankers and analysts are like carnival barkers: They are loud, colorful, and sometimes entertaining, but they care only about how much money you will make for them.

At times it's difficult to develop a return on investment based on customer evangelism tactics, such as helping the community and hiring genuinely happy and pleasant customer service representatives. (Indeed, employee evangelism can be a central component to customer evangelism, and if that's a vantage point you wish to explore, we suggest that while you read this book you replace the word "customer" with "employee.") It may be rather difficult to empirically prove ahead of time that focusing on word of mouth as a conduit for improved sales will actually work, just as it may be difficult to prove that spending $1.4 million on a Super Bowl commercial will result in a four-fold rise in sales or that a broker will improve the wealth of your financial portfolio. All are calculated leaps of faith. But organizational leaders who steadfastly believe that building relationships with customers and finding pathways to inspire them are believing in themselves as an agent of change. Even though evidence abounds that word of mouth is the most trusted form of media and the deciding factor for trying new products and services, it's still far from being the most employed form of marketing. We need more confident change agents like you to change the world of marketing.

CHAPTER THREE

Customer Plus-Delta

*Opportunities are often missed because we are broadcasting
when we should be listening.*

—Author unknown

As we searched for organizations that have created customer
evangelists, we looked at many types of companies and industries.
Whether it was small businesses or heavyweights in the Fortune
500, whether they sold directly to individual people or to other
businesses, each one taught us explicity that soliciting regular and
systematic feedback from customers is the fundamental, key component to creating customer evangelists. All of the companies we
studied know what their customers say about them. They encourage
customer participation and feedback. They respond to it and often
use it as the basis for compensating their employees. The methods
vary, but the intent is consistent: they have a strong desire and a systematic process to understand what customers love about them and
how they can improve. They have mastered the art of Customer
Plus-Delta: the first of the six tenets of customer evangelism.

Customer Plus-Delta is our term for gathering feedback. The
Plus indicates an understanding of what customers love, what they
talk about, or what most inspires them. The *Delta* symbolizes what

needs to be improved. Performing a Customer Plus-Delta at various customer touch points gathers quantitative and qualitative data about your organization's performance that can create a big-picture view of how your organization is really performing at the customer level.

Many of our profiled organizations receive hundreds or more e-mails or customer communications a day from customers, many of them filled with suggestions, complaints, and praise. Overwhelming? No way, say the leaders we talked with. They wouldn't have it any other way. To them, a deluge of e-mail confirms that their customers really care. Almost every marketing person agrees that customer input is important. It is (or should be) the basis for many of your organization's strategic decisions. However, ask most marketers if they routinely gather feedback, and many times the answer is, "We don't have enough money in our budget to do market research." It seems the prevailing opinion on performing customer research is that it costs a lot of money, takes a lot of time, and requires too many resources. Common customer feedback tactics include focus groups, customer satisfaction surveys, comment cards, ethnographic studies, qualitative research, and quantitative research. For many organizations, these tactics require considerable work, resources, and time. We discovered with our case story companies that gathering continuous customer feedback is easier and less expensive than you might think.

The most customer-oriented organizations use deceptively simple tactics to understand what customers are thinking. They understand the domino effect of customer satisfaction. Research conducted in the 1980s and 1990s by TARP, a customer loyalty research firm, shows that satisfied customers tell an average of five to eight people about their experience with a company or a product; dissatisfied customers tell 10 to 16 people.[1] For some perspective, let's use TARP's formula to understand the exponential potential of unhappy customers. We'll use the lower ranges for argument's sake. Let's say you have 1,000 customers whose satisfaction you gauge using a survey tool.

How to Measure the Buzz of Happy and Unhappy Customers

Total number of customers	1,000
% of satisfied customers	62%, or 620
Satisfied referrals	620 × 5
Total Happy Referrals	3,100
% of dissatisfied customers	38%, or 380
Dissatisfied referrals	380 × 10
Total Unhappy Referrals	3,800

This chart shows that more than one-half of the referrals for a company can be negative, even though only one-third of its customers are dissatisfied. With the Internet, these results can be significantly higher. Web sites such as *epinions.com* and *planetfeedback.com* are entirely dedicated to encouraging customers to spread the word, often negatively, about any organization. Often, a marketer's perception is that customers are satisfied if they do not complain, but this perception can mask a more common phenomenon: inertia.

Why then don't unhappy customers complain? It's hard. It takes time. They may be uncomfortable delivering criticism, or they don't expect results from their efforts. Silent, unhappy customers eventually dump you, never to call again. TARP found that for every person who complains, there are 26 who don't. Disappoint or anger enough of those 26 and a few may become vigilante customers. Suddenly it's their mission to besmirch your name whenever the opportunity arises.

Organizations that practice Customer Plus-Delta value customer feedback. For them, Customer Plus-Delta is more than a series of discrete activities; it's a philosophy extolled by a company's leaders through front-line employees. It's bound by a set of rules that makes many of the tried-and-true standards of market research obsolete.

There are 10 golden rules of Customer Plus-Delta:

1. Believe that customers possess good ideas.

2. Gather customer feedback at every opportunity.

3. Focus on continual improvement.

4. Actively solicit good and bad feedback.

5. Don't spend vast sums of money doing it.

6. Seek real-time feedback.

7. Make it easy for customers to provide their feedback (in person, by e-mail, through Web sites, at conferences).

8. Leverage technology to aid your efforts.

9. Share customer feedback throughout the organization.

10. Use input to make changes—and communicate changes back to customers.

As a strategy, Customer Plus-Delta builds loyal and more profitable customers. When customers feel they are being listened to by companies, they spread positive (and unsolicited) word of mouth. That's the finding of Communispace, a Watertown, Massachusetts, company that creates and manages private, branded online communities for companies. Communispace surveyed 2,196 members of their clients communities—20 communities representing 15 companies. They found that 82 percent of community members said they were more likely to recommend the company's products than before joining the community. Furthermore, they found that 54 percent of community members were more inclined to purchase products from the company since joining the community.[2]

Customer Plus-Delta improves the quality of products and services. Customers will only evangelize products and services they love and believe in. Compliments and complaints from current and departing customers create opportunities for improvement. But regular and systematic feedback systems help strengthen emotional bonds. Think about the last time a company asked for your feedback. Can you remember? When it actually happens, you may say to yourself, "Wow. They value my opinion. I appreciate being asked." An ongoing relationship and dialogue with customers about understanding their opinions shows that you care. Don't assume customers wish to be left alone; if you're not sure, ask for their permission. Like karma, goodwill is returned tenfold.

Customer Plus-Delta saves time and money. Launching new products and services can be expensive, time-consuming, and risky. Validating new concepts with customers can mitigate a sizable number of large-scale risks. Before you purchase raw materials, before you finalize manufacturing and delivery processes, before you finalize the sales literature and pitches, ask your existing customers to weigh in with their opinions. Let them spot trouble points, and encourage them to be critical. You'll add to the buzz that you are a customer-centered company. Your customers will tell their friends, colleagues, and family that you value their feedback. Positive comments can become part of your marketing. You can document the positive comments you receive and use them as testimonials in your brochures, on your Web site, and in your PR efforts.

As a reader of this book, chances are you've completed more than your fair share of customer satisfaction surveys. "Did we meet your needs? Yes or No. What is your perception of our service? Rate us 1 to 5," etc. These surveys can provide helpful information about what customers think, but if they're too long—which they usually are—the results are not often what we really need. Similarly in service industries, the mechanical question often heard in restaurants,

"How is everything today?" usually elicits the perfunctory "Fine," without really thinking about it. When this standard question is asked without real interest by the restaurant, the exercise is a waste of time. To really understand what customers think, it helps to dig deeper yet keep it simple.

- Do they recommend your product, brand, or company? (Yes, No, Don't know.)

- If *yes*, why? Do customers *love* something about your product, brand, or company?

- What's the one thing they value the most about your product, brand, or company?

- What do they say when they recommend you to others?

- If *no* or *don't know*, why? What must you improve to earn their recommendation?

- When was the last time you angered or disappointed them?

In the customer evangelism model, it's pretty simple: Customers either recommend you, or they do not. It's rather binary. Yes or No. *Don't know* is pretty close to a *No*. Since most surveys are overly long and complicated, a short survey that's to the point is easier to complete and will provide better response rates.

W/M Display, a company that creates and manufactures point-of-sale (POS) displays for use in retail stores, understands the benefits of Customer Plus-Delta.

Paul Scriba, president of the 50-year-old company, wanted to understand how his customers, who manufacture everything from chewing gum to lawn mowers, perceived his products, so he engaged Sloane Communications to find out. Instead of devising a paper-based, quantitative survey filled with a daunting list of multiple-choice questions to grade dubious levels of satisfaction,

Sloane conducted journalistic-style interviews with W/M Display's customers over the telephone. The interviews revealed that W/M's customers thought the displays were of high quality, and they were impressed with W/M's collaborative and creative approach to solving its retail marketing challenges. By digging deeper than any survey could, however, Sloane discovered stories of value, such as these:

- A display for a major mass merchandiser that increased sales 30 percent

- Product introduction support that helped the product become a sales leader in its category

- Innovative ideas that helped clients sell shelf space and key accounts

- Designs that increased display flexibility and reduced costs by 25 percent

Historically, W/M had positioned itself as a manufacturer of high-quality POS displays, but customer interviews indicated that W/M provided even more. Customers considered the value of W/M's process—studying how consumers purchase, examining store environments, and exploring what individual retailers require and prefer from merchandising programs—as valuable as the results produced.

Sloane worked with W/M to reposition it as a services firm that helps customers increase retail sales. With this new positioning, W/M remodeled its sales process, refined its sales conversations, and created brochures that showcase results—helping differentiate itself from competitors even more. The results? "Our sales are up 25 percent annually," Scriba says. "We have added a third shift to keep up with production."[3]

It's impossible for us to prescribe specific tactics for every business and product. What works for a consumer packaged goods company is not necessarily applicable to a law firm focusing on employment law. We have included strategy analyses from our case-study companies and others as foundation practices to use as a beginning point for understanding how much customers love you.

1. Make real customer contact. Take at least one customer to breakfast or lunch every week. Ask as many questions as you can think of, letting the customer do most of the talking. Sounds easy enough, right? Funny how fast our schedules fill up with company—not customer—meetings. Customers are more important than anything else that could possibly be going on inside your company. That's the approach of Herb Kelleher. Well known as the Wild Turkey–drinking, Harley-Davidson–riding, maverick chairman of Southwest Airlines, Kelleher is a thoughtful company leader who regularly listens to what customers have to say. When he was CEO, he routinely flew on Southwest's planes as a pseudo–flight attendant, handing out peanuts and sitting with customers to talk with them. JetBlue founder and CEO (and ex-Southwest executive) David Neeleman is known to do this as well. Mark Cuban, owner of the Dallas Mavericks, attends almost every game—home and away—and sits with fans in the seats, not in a skybox. Sometimes he sits with fans in the $8 seats, talking with them and experiencing the games as they do. His mission is to discover what's working and how he can improve their experience.

2. Scour the Web. Use the latest and greatest search engine to discover what people say about you on fan sites, in the newsgroups, on blogs, and on e-mail discussion lists. Google News Alerts and *Technorati.com*'s Watchlists service will send alerts anytime a keyword (say your product or company) name is mentioned online. Understanding the word of mouth online helps you discover—and quickly contend with—any customer vigilantes.

Firms use Web lurkers for customer service

by Chris Woodyard, *USA TODAY,* February 6, 2002

His name evokes a menacing image. The Lurker. The Starwood Lurker.

Every workday, the Lurker trolls the Internet. He dips into frequent-traveler electronic bulletin boards to check the postings about his employer, Starwood Hotels & Resorts. He ferrets out comments on any of the big hotel chains that operate under Starwood's corporate umbrella—Westin, Sheraton, St. Regis, or W. And when he finds them: Zap—he strikes. He dispatches an e-mail to the sender or posts his own message on the electronic bulletin board. Chat room prowlers such as the Starwood Lurker have become common on the Internet. Hotel and airline representatives are increasingly showing up on travel bulletin boards to answer questions or clear up misunderstandings.

They have to. It's one thing when a customer writes or phones in a complaint to a company. It's quite another when the same customer posts a critical e-mail for all the world to see. What makes Starwood's Lurker special is that his work is now a full-time job. Offline, his name is William Sanders.

He isn't some college-age technogeek. Sanders describes himself, at 47, as the "old guy on the team" and so uncomfortable with technology that "I can't even complete a conference call." Sanders himself lurks in Austin, Texas, where his official title is specialist in the e-communications department. He's a relative newcomer to electronic bulletin boards, as is Starwood.

The hotel company, like so many others, has quietly watched for months as frequent travelers write missives about their favorite or least favorite hotels, tips about accumulating frequent-traveler points, and the like. The most closely monitored of these boards is FlyerTalk, a feature on *InsideFlyer.com,* which is visited by many frequent travelers. It's considered a powerhouse in the travel industry, with 300,000 visitors a month who generally stay 15 to 30 minutes. Within the FlyerTalk area are individual bulletin boards for each major airline and hotel chain.

Starwood officials say they saw plenty of opportunities to jump into the online conversation, but were reluctant. They say they didn't want to look like they were muscling in on free speech. But once the company made its first posting in the Starwood area of FlyerTalk's bulletin board December 1, the reaction was surprisingly positive. "Starwood rocks!" wrote a contributor in a post to the site 27 minutes after Starwood announced that it would participate there. "It's nice to have a travel company that actually cares about its customers," chimed in another.

"Within minutes of posting the first message under Starwood Preferred Guest, other people on the board started saying, 'It's pretty good you're helping him out,'" says Klaus Buellesbach, global director of customer service.

Since then, Starwood has joined in conversation "sparingly," preferring instead to try to reach anyone who posts a problem through private e-mail.

Monitoring the site became such a top priority that it was deemed essential to find someone who could handle it full time. In came Sanders, plucked from the relatively obscure ranks of customer complaint responders.

Sanders loves lurking.

Instead of getting chewed out over the phone all day as he did in his former job, Sanders says he now remedies travel headaches of hotel guests in the anonymity of cyberspace. "The people here are more savvy," he says.

Sanders spends most of his workday perusing the messages posted on the Starwood site. He also checks the bulletin boards of about a dozen other hotel chains to check for references to Starwood. He has gotten to know his counterparts at competing hotel chains such as Hilton, which have their own lurkers performing the same task.

Sanders is even making a few online friends among the travelers. One Germany-based traveler messages him about every three weeks to mope about how a particular Sheraton never opened in Malaysia.

David Goldsmith says he didn't stay at Starwood hotels two years ago. But after having had good experiences there, room upgrades and other perks that go with elite frequent-stay status, he says Starwood—and the Lurker—have made him a believer.

And Randy Petersen, the frequent-flier mile expert who runs InsideFlyer, says he thinks the lurkers serve a purpose.

"Customer service is, in theory, about listening and resolving issues with your customers," he says. "In this case, FlyerTalk has become a bit of a surrogate center for that to take place." Sanders is gratified to hear things like that. He sees himself as a fixer.

"It's another way to exceed the expectations of the people who are staying with us," the Lurker says. "That's what it's all about."

© 2002, USA TODAY. Reprinted with permission.

3. Gather feedback on your Web site. A page on your organization's Web site should encourage customers to provide feedback. Make it easy to find the area from anywhere on your site. Collect data for every type of feedback: product complaints, customer service questions, franchising inquiries, and employment questions.

If you want to know what's working well for customers, include an option allowing them to submit their "love" letters, personal stories, and photos of themselves with your product. Feature those stories on your Web site and in your marketing materials. Bicycle manufacturer Bike Friday consistently makes its customers the stars of its marketing efforts. Many times the customers willingly provide their e-mail addresses in the marketing materials. Prospects can contact the customer directly for a referral. A blog can be a very valuable feedback tool, especially among customers who closely follow the company's activities. Engage customers with posts that ask questions about product usage or service issues. Keep the conversation going in the comments on each blog post.

4. Mine call center data. Be religious about going through call center logs. Some companies receive hundreds of calls every day. That's hundreds of opportunities for customers to express their love or to make a suggestion. Look for trends. Talk with your call center team often. Listen in on calls every month. Nestlé USA found that just 20 percent of the calls to the company's call center

were complaints. Many callers were suggesting how to improve the company's products, so managers began to return the calls of these opinionated customers. Based on the suggestions, Nestlé improved the packaging for its Coffee-mate product and saw a significant jump in sales.[4]

5. End every customer meeting with feedback. For anyone who meets with customers in person, use a visual Plus-Delta tool like the one pictured in Figure 3.1. At the conclusion of meetings, ask customers to list what worked well in the meeting; those items go in the Plus column. Then ask customers what could be improved next time; those items go in the Delta column. Tell your participants that the session has no right or wrong answers and that it's not a time for debate. Instead, it's an opportunity for honest, immediate feedback on the service just delivered. The beauty of the Plus-Delta tool is that it is a five-minute brainstorming session. At your next meeting with the customer, open with how you have addressed the deltas raised at the last meeting. Plus-Delta can work for phone meetings, too.

Figure 3.1 | Create Your Own Plus-Delta

Ask your audience for feedback in short, bumper-stickered encapsulations. Encourage feedback from everyone, especially within groups.

Plus	Delta
What was beneficial?	What can be improved?

6. Interview your customers. This is not the same as conducting focus groups. Ask an independent third party to perform in-depth in-person or phone interviews to capture what customers really think. Work with customers to understand the value of your products and how they describe your organization's value proposition and product offerings.

7. Use online surveys. Web surveys allow you to get feedback quickly and cost-effectively. Mix in a few open-ended questions that help you get a better picture of how your customers feel about you. Try questions such as, "What one thing do you value most about our company?" You'll get amazing answers that you can use in your marketing materials; your ad agency would never have been able to dream up such genuine and insightful copy. Chicago's WBEZ is the third largest public radio station in the country. It has 550,000 listeners and 45,000 members—loyal customers, if you will—who support the station's programming with financial contributions.

A 15-member Listener Advisory Council provides WBEZ feedback on how the station is fulfilling its mission, which is to serve the community. This is no easy task; the Chicagoland area is home to roughly seven million people. Gathering data is a challenge for a volunteer group with no budget. Before 2002, the Listener Advisory Council usually conducted in-person surveys using volunteers at events. It was a time-intensive process; data had to be manually entered into a computer for analysis. At one point, the council considered calling listeners at home for feedback, but without a budget to hire a polling firm, many volunteers would be needed. The negatives associated with calling people at home outweighed the benefits. Finally, a new plan was devised: take advantage of the reach and efficiency of the Internet by using a Web-based survey. In January 2002, the station launched a 12-question survey. Respondents were asked a series of multiple-choice questions about on-air programming and listening habits. Two open-ended questions asked:

- What is the one thing you value the most about Chicago Public Radio?

- If you could suggest one thing Chicago Public Radio could do to improve its service to the community, what would that be?

Sent once to the station's in-house e-mail list, the survey generated more than 800 responses in two weeks. Hundreds of suggestions poured in, from better traffic reporting and additional coverage of local political news to improving the station's fundraising efforts. Responses were informative, constructive, often passionate, and even included some 150-word essays.

Many answers, like the following, were a marketer's dream.

- "[WBEZ] treats me like a person with a brain . . . gives me something to think about, helps me explore the issues of the day."

- "Since listening to [WBEZ], I have become well informed, better educated, and a more aware person. I did not finish college but am able to participate in conversations with the most intelligent people around because of [WBEZ]. People are often amazed that I can discuss politics, the economy, world affairs, etc. Not because they think I am not bright, but because I have knowledge that many people do not."

- "I feel a sense of community with the producers of the programming and the staff at WBEZ and the other listeners. You are my neighborhood. I feel at home whenever WBEZ is on."

Suggested improvements included:

- "The 'Chicago Matters' series on the public schools was absolutely amazing. More programming in that vein would be great."

- "One day a week, maybe Wednesday during AM and PM drives, have an events bulletin board (so there might still be time to plan on going) dealing with museums, music opportunities, festivals, etc."

- "When you have 'experts' on discussing public housing, why not one of us who lives there? More inside information."

- "Traffic reports are usually not timely. By the time they report an accident, it has usually been cleared up."[5]

Procter & Gamble spends about $150 million annually on consumer research. It used to have a serious addiction to focus groups, with each session costing more than $25,000. In 2001, the consumer products giant decided to break its focus-group dependence and turn to the Internet for feedback; its online tools gather instantaneous consumer feedback about products on the drawing board and current products on store shelves. Barbara Lindsey, P&G's director of consumer research services, says that the company had devoted about half of its research budget to online feedback. Using traditional methods, a simple consumer survey might take three or four weeks and cost as much as $50,000, whereas an Internet survey can be completed in ten days at a cost of $10,000. In effect, P&G discovered that Web-based feedback is five times cheaper and produces data four times faster.

"It can save you a whole lot of time and a whole lot of money," Lindsey says.[6]

8. Create a customer advisory board. Ask your best customers to meet with you, physically or virtually, so they can provide feedback

on a regular basis. You'll be surprised at how many of them jump at the chance to be on an advisory board.

In April 2001, *washingtonpost.com,* the Internet version of the *Washington Post,* invited its readers to join a volunteer advisory panel; over 15,000 people signed up within two months. Thirty-nine percent of the panelists live in the Washington, D.C., area, and 55 percent are spread among 30 different states. The remaining 9 percent of the panelists are scattered among ten different countries. "The online panel gives us a way to conduct product testing," says Alex Johnston, senior research analyst at Washington-Post.Newsweek Interactive who oversees the readers' group. "With the panel, we get results quicker—in a couple of weeks—compared with previous methods of product testing. We can make changes to existing products faster and react more quickly."[7]

The newspaper has used the panel for many different purposes, including:

- Product testing for the personalized news product, *mywashingtonpost.com:* Panel feedback helps the online staff understand the value of existing and new services and how to improve current marketing efforts.

- Testing of new ad formats: *washingtonpost.com* tests new advertising products for readers' reactions. While many readers typically frown on new advertising, Johnston says his team gathered important insights from the panel.

- Evaluation of special sections: Following the events of September 11, the panel was asked to give feedback about the way coverage was presented on the Web site. As a result, site staff had a better understanding of what held the greatest interest for most readers, and designers made adjustments accordingly.

- General perception testing: The panel has participated in an online redesign effort. Surveys ask readers about their connection with various sections, which sections they would like to
see more of, and how they would like them to be presented.

The Internet and advances in technology have made interacting
with customers easier and less expensive. Technology allows us to know
our customers in ways we never could have before. Maxine Clark,
founder and "chief executive bear" of retailer Build-A-Bear Workshop, says that every company should embrace the instantaneous
feedback the Internet delivers. "The Internet has been a huge, huge,
positive impact on retailing in general," she says. "Customers expect
you to have it as an option for them. And they want it for all kinds
of things, whether it's complaining about the business, telling you
good things about the business, buying things. People want to give
their e-mail address . . . [it's] a way for them to get instant communication and know what is going on."[8]

How organizations act on the free advice of customers differen-
tiates them from competitors. Organizations focused on creating
customer evangelists exhibit a willingness to share their knowledge
with customers, business partners, and their industry. As we outline
in the next chapter, it's a phenomenon we call Napsterizing your
knowledge.

Napsterize Your Knowledge

Information wants to be free.[1]

—Stewart Brand

When 19-year-old programmer and college dropout Shawn Fanning wrote a computer program in 1999 to help his roommate find and share MP3 music files, the program allowed Web surfers to open their hard drives to other people and do the same. He named his program Napster, a nickname given to him years earlier. In 18 months the world of computing and knowledge-sharing changed. Word of Napster spread like an enormous, worldwide virus. Napster quickly became home to a community of 58 million people who shared about 9.4 million files with one another every day. It didn't take long for the lawyers to get involved; based on a suit brought by the Recording Industry Association of America (RIAA) and a number of record companies, Judge Marilyn Hall Patel of U.S. district court ordered Napster, six months before the company's two-year anniversary, to halt the trading of music files. Backed by the RIAA, the American legal system killed Napster.

The RIAA argued that Napster was stealing millions of dollars from its bank account because people were obtaining songs for free stead of paying $17.95 for full-length CDs. Record companies had long wielded an iron hand over how customers used their intellectual property, and Napster wasn't about to change that. Record companies said they controlled standards and distribution; Napster strayed on to its turf, and it deserved to be whacked. Having one's intellectual property "Napsterized" was suddenly giving other industries fits, namely big media companies. Movie studios, television production companies, and book publishers feared they were next. Once something is digitized, all it needs is a distribution system to spread easily, and that's what Napster delivered.

The widespread and sometimes overwrought fear of getting Napsterized was evident with the appearance of a February 5, 2001, article in the *National Underwriter*, a publication for the insurance and financial services industry. It warned that time was running out for the technologically challenged insurance industry because it shared the same risk factors with the entertainment industry: a highly regulated market, products based on information, a few dominant sellers without real competition, and a large number of customers with no easy way to self-organize. The article argued that Napster-like clones would put the industry on a "hit list" and eventually "shake [the industry] to its roots with an alternative e-business model."[2]

National Underwriter's argument had it partly right: Napster-like clones can shake up an industry by providing faster and more efficient models to share and distribute information. The models also make sampling highly efficient; in fact, Napster was the best try-before-you-buy model ever created. Consider what happened to record sales before, during, and after Napster. In 2000, with the service in full swing, record sales were up 4 percent, according to SoundScan, a company that tracks record sales. After Judge Patel shut Napster down in early 2001, record sales for that year declined 5 percent. In fact, this was the first time in SoundScan's ten-year history that music sales decreased. Although it's possible that such factors as competition, rising prices, changing demographics, or a lack of anything worth buying could have affected sales, a June 2000 study by Yankelovich Partners confirms Napster's positive effect. The research firm found that among the 16,000 Americans it surveyed, 59 percent who downloaded music said that they later bought the CD. It seems that Napster stimulated sales because it created bite-size chunks of otherwise expensive CDs. After all, consumer packaged-good companies like P&G and Unilever have successfully made small boxes of soap, laundry detergent, and just about every product found in a box available for years as an inducement to consumers to buy. Why not music? Joel Selvin, the San Francisco *Chronicle's* pop music editor, says that "Napster encouraged people to try new music they wouldn't necessarily spend money to check out."[3] Napster has since been reincarnated as a paid service in which digital songs are "rented" by the month. But it is Napster's early period of meteoric growth, entirely through word of mouth, that is worth examining for marketers.

The grassroots growth of Napster's peer-to-peer network indicates the makings of a new type of distribution channel and value proposition. Companies that share their intellectual property and business processes with customers and partners increase the perceived and actual value of their products and services. This axiom is proven by SolutionPeople, a creativity and consulting firm. It makes its knowledge available in a handheld tool and in the way it conducts its creativity workshops. A competitor could conceivably take the company's ideas and processes and copy them, but SolutionPeople has proven since its launch in 1989 that success comes from consistently strong execution. Southwest Napsterized its flight schedule by making it fully viewable on its Web site. In 2001, that level of transparency was far beyond what other airlines did; most kept their schedules a closely guarded secret so that they could charge higher fares. With Southwest leading the way, now most airline schedules follow the Southwest model; they are more transparent and fully viewable online. It was Southwest's Napsterization that led the way. Mark Cuban, the owner of the Dallas Mavericks, is a frequent blogger.

He covers a variety of subjects, but once or twice per week he discusses his team, the rationale for trades, the NBA, and other topics of interest to the team's fans. He's Napsterizing his knowledge by becoming his own publisher. His openness creates both fans and detractors, but Cuban would rather strengthen the relationship with existing fans by sharing his knowledge and opinions than worry about disagreements caused by his blog posts on basketball matters. Tim O'Reilly is another frequent blogger. Like Cuban, he blogs about a range of subjects, some of which are related to the business of his company. It's our contention that his blog and its Napsterizing effects have significantly raised his profile and, by extension, his company's profile. Like Cuban, he has his detractors but he has plenty of fans, too. That's the trade-off when it comes to creating and maintaining passion. It goes both ways.

Companies that Napsterize their knowledge in the marketplace tend to enjoy a marketplace response of help and intellectual capital improvements. For marketers, Napster's rapid growth and influence teach at least five key lessons.

1. Making intellectual property widely available can open avenues for new products and services.

2. The Internet and peer-to-peer technology used in Napster allow information to be shared and passed to others at light speed.

3. The creation of new technology is unending; marketers must continue to adapt and innovate to ride the waves of opportunity that new technologies bring.

4. Customers expect open platforms and try-before-you-buy models.

5. Customers like to join communities to share and exchange data on a one-to-one or one-to-many level.

Napster-like models have the potential to bring about wholesale changes in marketing strategies, company strategies, and perhaps entire industries. Napster-like entrants are good for the marketplace: they prompt industries to reassess their market position and, ultimately, their value to customers. In the end, Napsterizing has a positive effect; Napsterizing your knowledge widens the information portal to your customers. Napsterization allows stronger ownership of your product or service, thereby making it easier for customers to share with friends and colleagues.

Spurred by the success of Napster-like distribution as well as the open source software movement, individuals and companies in several industries have initiated major plays to disseminate their intellectual capital across multiple channels.

The Software Industry

Web server software is what makes Web sites accessible. The most widely used Web server software is not made by Microsoft, IBM, or Sun. It's Apache, and it's free. In 1995 a group of programmers worked together to fix Rob McCool's popular (yet "buggy") software known as an HTTP (HyperText Transfer Protocol) server. The resulting program was called Apache because it was "A-patchy" server. In 1999, the programmers formed the Apache Software Foundation to provide organizational, legal, and financial support for Apache Server. In 2006, free Apache commanded 62 percent of the Web server market, according to Netcraft.

Finnish programmer Linus Torvalds created the Linux operating system in 1991. Several years later, Linux had grown and matured thanks to several thousand volunteer programmers across the world. Linux is now supported by industry giants IBM and Oracle. According to IDC, an information technology (IT) research firm, Linux commanded 31 percent of the server market in 2006.

The Education Industry

In 2001, the Massachusetts Institute of Technology (MIT) decided to make its entire curriculum—lecture notes, assignments, sample problems, reading lists for 1,800 courses—freely available on the Internet. Each faculty member decides on the amount of content to share, but there are no passwords. No monthly subscription. It's free for everyone. That's a $104,000 value. Why would one of the world's top learning institutions give away its intellectual property? Because an institute committee tasked with studying the impact of the Internet in 1999 decided that the best way to advance an MIT-style education would be to widen the access to its knowledge. By making access free, MIT's knowledge would spread exponentially via word of mouth through the networks of its visitors. An education virus, if you will. MIT wants to push the frontiers of its knowledge by giving other researchers the chance to increase the universe of knowledge. MIT president Charles M. Vest says the initiative, dubbed MIT OpenCourseWare, "expresses our belief in the way education can be advanced—by constantly widening access to information and by inspiring others to participate."[5]

OpenCourseWare hosts about a million visitors per month. Five years after its launch, OpenCourseWare has taught MIT plenty about the consumption of educational materials and the volunteerism it can inspire. Volunteers have translated course materials into 15 languages. Educators from other institutions report they are using MIT's accessible courses as benchmarks and standards against which to measure their own courses. It's brought faculty closer: two 30-year MIT faculty members had never met nor were they aware they were teaching work that was similar until the CourseWare project led them to discover one another.

MIT's strategy at the outset was to present the value of its intellectual capital as an up-front offering; the university was betting it would lead smart high school students to their door for the "experience" of interacting with top-notch students and researchers. That strategy appears to have paid off. Project director Anne Margulies says students who enroll formally at MIT report that Open-CourseWare was what first attracted them to the institution and gave them an idea of what to expect in intellectual rigor and homework. It was a great try-before-you-buy program. On the opposite end of the student experience, MIT alumni initially opposed Open-CourseWare because they thought it would devalue their degree; Margulies says that resistance changed because the project allows them free access to continuing education.

One of the less-quantifiable aspects of MIT's project is the unprecedented expressions of enthusiasm of its fans. Margulies says, "It's truly overwhelming to receive the amount of fan mail we receive every day (over 10,000 e-mails so far). Some 90 percent of the e-mail we receive is to thank us for sharing MIT's content . . . and we respond to every single message." [6]

The Publishing Industry

In 2000, author Seth Godin wrote *Unleashing the Ideavirus,* a book whose premise is that an engaging idea can travel through the Internet like a fast-moving virus. To prove his point, he released *Unleashing the Ideavirus* as an e-book on his Web site, *www.ideavirus .com,* encouraging readers to download it for free and tell friends about it. A hardcover version was also available, but for $40. One of the book's mottos: "The more you give away, the more it's worth." The results were telling: 400,000 readers downloaded the book in the first 30 days of its release, making it the most read e-book ever. Eventually, the book was downloaded more than 1 million times because friends told friends about Godin's book, and the hardcover version reached number five on Amazon's bestseller list.

Amazon publicly ranks sales of its products, which helps customers understand the relative popularity of the book they are about to purchase. The charts help publishers and authors track a book's popularity by the hour; when a book appears one hour on a nationally syndicated radio program, you can watch the Amazon sales skyrocket the next hour. O'Reilly & Associates, a publisher of technology titles, developed special software to check the Amazon rankings daily and alert O'Reilly to the movement of its titles and those of its competitors.

The Professional Services Industry

Mayer, Brown, Rowe & Maw, the tenth largest law firm in the world, develops and hosts free Web sites that provide information on legal specialties. The firm hosts sites like *Securitization.net,* a free online resource for information on structured finance. The site helps industry members stay current on global structured finance developments from a growing list of industry participants who regularly provide commentary, news, rating criteria, accounting regulation analyses, legal analyses, and deal descriptions. The site even features content from a competing firm. It does not loudly brandish the Mayer, Brown, Rowe & Maw logo, and only a small link at the bottom of the front page mentions the firm. By spearheading a comprehensive portal, or hub of information, about a specific topic, the law firm subtly positions itself as a leader in the area of structured finance.

As the widespread adoption of the Linux operating system has shown, Napsterizing one's intellectual efforts can help create an industry standard. Napsterized knowledge means wider acceptance of products and services, which leads to more word of mouth and buzz. How buzz is concocted and spread is the focus of our next chapter.

CHAPTER FIVE

Build the Buzz

Buzz is not about elegant advertising or glitzy tradeshows.
It's about what customers—the people who pay for products—
tell each other.

—**Emanuel Rosen**, author of *The Anatomy of Buzz*

Buzz is the pathway that helps shepherd new customers toward you. Each wave of buzz provides your evangelists with another reason to extol you. Buzz helps people discover your business faster than do traditional marketing programs. It helps your salespeople develop relationships, because prospects already have some knowledge of your product. In some cases, buzz sells the product by itself.

To understand buzz is to appreciate its influence. Consulting firm McKinsey & Company estimates that 67 percent of the U.S. economy is influenced by buzz. Aside from the industries most associated with buzz, such as entertainment and fashion, McKinsey cites finance, travel, publishing, automotive, pharmaceuticals, and even agriculture as industries that are significantly influenced by buzz.

What is buzz? Emanuel Rosen, the dean of buzz, wrote the book (literally) on understanding how it works; *The Anatomy of Buzz* dissects the launch points, trajectories, and communication systems that fuel buzz. Rosen began his quest for buzz knowledge in the late 1990s, when he was in charge of marketing for a Silicon

Valley software company that had yet to release its product. Called EndNote, it's a software tool that helps researchers and authors keep track of their references and compile bibliographies for their research papers and books. One day, before the product was even ready, a purchase order arrived from Princeton University in New Jersey.

"It really shocked me," Rosen says. "Suddenly someone from the outside world recognizes it. It's weird. You have this feeling of Wow! It's actually happening."[1] Even though only a handful of people in the world were supposed to know about the product at the time, EndNote had good buzz.

Is buzz different from word of mouth? Yes. Word of mouth is "mainly face-to-face communication," Rosen says, when two people share information or opinions with one another.

"Listen, you have to see the movie *A Beautiful Mind* that I saw yesterday. Have you seen it?" he asks, suddenly as we sit with Rosen in his adopted home of Palo Alto, California. "Not yet," we say. "You really have to see it. OK?" For several minutes we discuss the film's attributes, its leading man, Russell Crowe, and Crowe's previous work. We share a moment of connection. "So this is a comment that went from my brain to your brain, and when you add up all the comments that travel among people at a certain point in time about *A Beautiful Mind*, that's the buzz about it," Rosen says.[2]

Buzz includes the multitude of conversations that exist in person and on the Web in chat rooms, online bulletin boards, blogs, and forwarded e-mails. As Rosen defines it, buzz is "the aggregate of all person-to-person communication about a particular product, service, or company at any point in time."[3] Taking that into account, we say:

Buzz = Word of Mouth + Word of Mouse

Marketers love buzz because it can hurtle a product into the stratosphere of the highly visible. Products that have hit earth like an attention-getting asteroid are a testament to the mystery of buzz: Beanie Babies, Razor Scooters, Palm handheld organizers, iPods, *The Blair Witch Project*. To become a practiced buzz marketer, one must understand that buzz travels over invisible networks. Pick up an in-flight magazine and examine the airline's flight paths. Among the paths you'll see hubs, where flights originate and end. Imagine the hubs as people and the flight paths as connections between people. Buzz travels through these connections via face-to-face meetings, the Internet, phone calls, and the like. Rosen's term for buzz-spreaders is *hubs*. Hubs are trusted sources of information who disseminate information quickly. There are two types of hubs:

1. Megahubs. They are often writers at newspapers, like the *Wall Street Journal*'s technology columnist Walt Mossberg, or television personalities like Jon Stewart, both of whom have developed strong followings and whose opinion can wield significant influence among their audiences. They are prominent politicians like Bill Clinton, who was still making news years after being out of office based on his work for victims of Hurricane Katrina and the Asian tsunami. Oprah Winfrey is such a megahub that she almost deserves a special category. A product's appearance on her show is almost guaranteed to crash a company's servers, tax the phone banks, propel a product to best-seller status, and cause a run on inventory.

2. Network hubs. They are people in the community who can influence a sizable network of coworkers, friends, and family—people in your office who always seem to know the latest movie, fashion, or gadget. They may not have sizable audiences like Oprah, but they are trusted sources of information, like church pastors, community council members, school board presidents, or chamber executives.

What causes buzz to spread among the megahubs and the network hubs?

Some products are "contagious," meaning that people are "infected" with the idea of the product just by seeing it in use by someone else. Products or services with high visibility cause buzz. Personal digital assistants like the Palm Pilot, the Motorola StarTac cell phone, and a number of the early digital cameras were naturally contagious because they were used in public places. It's hard not to engage in a conversation with someone who is using a sleek and sexy titanium Apple laptop computer. The hit HBO series *The Sopranos* was contagious because it's a brilliantly written show, and it's about people—colorful and unusual people. Our innate interest in other people prompts us to talk about them, especially if they are Mafia hoods. Buzz about a restaurant is often about the people who eat there. Movie buzz is often focused on the real-life actors in the film.

Taking that into account, how do you create customer evangelists by tapping in to network hubs?

- Be diligent in finding and tracking network hubs. Join the networking groups that your customers belong to. Find out who the "influencers" in these groups are, and form relationships with them.

- Target the hubs first with a new product or service; network hubs love to be the first to know something new.

- Bring the network hubs to forums where they can talk with others. For example, Apple holds twice yearly customer love-fests called MacWorld, where tens of thousands of company enthusiasts are courted by CEO Steve Jobs, renew old friendships, and wax about all things Macintosh.

- Devise ways to make sure others see hubs using your products. For example, PowerBar created a "PowerBar Elite" program. Athletes earn money when their picture appears in the media eating PowerBars or wearing PowerBar gear.

The principle idea is that individuals, not just the traditional megahubs, can help sell your product. Buzz-based programs that engage everyday influencers can be an addition (or a substitution) to the mass media approach that most PR firms employ. By talking directly with your customers, finding individual champions, and establishing relationships with the champions, you are on your way to creating good buzz.

There are myths about buzz. It's not the end-all as it is sometimes hyped to be. A *Harvard Business Review* article sheds light on this phenomenon, which the author calls "explosive self-generating demand." In "The Buzz on Buzz," author Renee Dye explains that before companies can take full advantage of buzz, executives must rid themselves of five common misconceptions about how buzz works, as shown in Figure 5.1.

Buzz sometimes arrive in ways you didn't expect or plan on. After his Dallas Mavericks experienced a frustrating loss to what he

Figure 5.1 | The Five Myths of Buzz

Myth	Reality
1. Only outrageous or edgy products are buzz worthy.	The most unlikely products, like prescription drugs, can generate tremendous buzz.
2. Buzz just happens.	Buzz is increasingly the result of shrewd marketing tactics in which companies seed a vanguard group, ration supplies, use celebrities to generate buzz, leverage the power of lists, and initiate grassroots marketing.
3. The best buzz starters are your best customers.	Often, a counterculture has a greater ability to start buzz.
4. To profit from buzz, you must act first and fast.	Copycat companies can reap substantial profits if they know when to jump in—and where not to.
5. The media and advertising are needed to create buzz.	When used too early or too much, the media and advertising can squelch buzz before it ignites.

Source: Renee Dye, "The Buzz on Buzz," *Harvard Business Review,* November-December 2000. (Reprinted with permission. © 2000 by the Harvard Business School Publishing Corporation; all rights reserved.)

considered poor officiating, Mark Cuban was quoted by the *Dallas Morning News* as saying of the NBA's director of officials, "Ed Rush might have been a great ref, but I wouldn't hire him to manage a Dairy Queen."[4] With one comment on January 8, 2002, an outspoken NBA owner launched a media frenzy that lasted several weeks. Cuban says his comment about not hiring the NBA's officiating chief to manage a Dairy Queen "just came out" during an interview with the newspaper. NBA commissioner David Stern was not pleased. He slapped Cuban with a $500,000 fine, the highest amount ever levied against an individual in professional sports. (Cuban matched the fine, as he does with all of the other fines he's received from the NBA, with a donation to charity.)

Stern's action generated untold amounts of buzz. Suddenly, fans and sports writers across the country squared off. Some writers called Cuban an overbearing loudmouth. NBA fan sites cheered Cuban for taking on "the system." Amateur NBA fan sites characterized Stern as a "soulless money-grubbing suit." All in all, it was high drama in the NBA, something the league hadn't seen since Michael Jordan's first retirement. Dairy Queen, proving itself to be as media savvy as Cuban, issued a challenge: perhaps Cuban should try managing a DQ for a day. A conventional professional sports team owner may have profusely apologized and donated money on behalf of DQ's favorite charity to settle the controversy. But Cuban quickly accepted DQ's challenge.

"It wasn't this preprogrammed marketing plan," Cuban told us during a night we chatted with him in Dallas. "Dairy Queen threw out the opportunity and I said, 'Why not have fun with it?' It's just on that checklist of life . . . I'd read from somebody who thought it was a good experience to work behind a service counter. There was a part of me that's always wanted to get a job at McDonald's to work for a couple weeks to get a reality check. When that opportunity came along, it was an opportunity for me to add a reality check to my list. And that's why when I got there, I took it seriously."[5]

So did the media. Cuban reported for work at a DQ store in Coppell, Texas, on January 16 at 6 AM, ready for training. Hundreds of people lined up to be the first for a Cuban-made Billionaire Blizzard. TV crews converged and helicopters flew overhead. Actor Tom Arnold showed up. Cuban appeared live from the store, with *Today Show* host Katie Couric, saying, "Welcome to Dairy Queen! May I take your order?" It was an event driven by buzz. The *Dallas Morning News* later reported that the publicity was worth nearly $5 million in equivalent advertising for the Mavericks and Dairy Queen. Reflecting on the experience a month after the mayhem had subsided, Cuban gives much of the credit to the company he maligned. "It was good for Dairy Queen—they're the ones that created the opportunity to make it good," Cuban says. "It was good for Paris Chapman, the local DQ guy, 'cause he made it good. It was good for me 'cause it was fun; it was a learning experience. It was good for the Mavs because we sold tickets there. People created a fun energy around it, and it made people realize that's what we sell. If what we're saying all along is about having fun, you gotta do fun things. You can't take yourself too seriously."[6]

There are several lessons to take away from Cuban's buzz-building experience:

- If you believe in something, fear not the controversy. Standing up for a cause that benefits a greater good will probably cause waves. But the waves inspire people to talk.

- If someone issues a challenge to you, take it. Have fun with it, and for God's sake, don't take yourself too seriously.

- Act quickly. If you see an opportunity to create good buzz, take it. It can be risky, but in the world of buzz, there are no compliments for caution.

- Be a little outrageous. If you let people see the real you, they feel as if they know you. Just as movie buzz is often about the real-life actors, people love to talk about others who put themselves on stage.

Buzz has a dark side. That's when companies try to manufacture it, or create fake buzz. "You like my car?" a good-looking, Banana Republic–clad, 20-something guy says near his car parked on a downtown street. "It's the new Ford Focus, and it's so money, dude! Here, have a Focus key chain." Customer evangelist? No, he's a hired poseur. Ford used a staged, Hollywood-style buzz approach in 2001 to launch the Ford Focus. Ford recruited a handful of trendy young adults in several cities to drive a Focus for six months. Their job was to hang out with the car in high-traffic areas and distribute Focus-themed trinkets to anyone who looked twice at the car. "We weren't looking for celebrities. We were looking for the assistants to celebrities, party planners, disc jockeys—the people who really seemed to influence what was cool," says Julie Roehm, Ford's marketing communication manager.[7]

To get Canadian consumers talking about Cheer laundry detergent, Procter & Gamble employed brightly outfitted "shoppers" to stage impromptu fashion shows in supermarkets. A July 2001 *Business Week* article described how the actors also happened to prominently mention that their colorful duds were washed in Cheer. Creating real customer evangelists through buzz takes work. Paying actors to pretend they are real evangelists is just a form of trickery.

"I don't think these more manipulative campaigns will go unnoticed by consumers," Renee Dye instructively says. "They're not stupid. The concept of street teams and other face-to-face initiatives may work for now, but in the long term, I think marketers will have to opt for more subtlety."[8]

As we mentioned earlier in the book, customer evangelism begins with a great product. But often it's how the product is experienced that generates the most buzz. Consider the difference between watching a professional basketball game on TV and watching a game in person. From the television experience, you might tell a friend about the outcome of the game and recount a spectacular play. From being at the game, you might tell a friend about any of these:

- The people in a booth outside the arena getting their heads shaved to resemble the team's star player

- How the announcer sounded like the "Let's get ready to rumble!" guy

- The free T-shirts shot out of air guns into the crowd during game breaks

- The cool hip-hop music played at the game

- How an entire section of the crowd received a coupon for a free Dairy Queen cone when the opponent's star player was "DQ'ed" (disqualified)

- The stylish team uniforms

- The skimpy cheerleaders' uniforms

- The crazy team owner cheering like a wild man on the sidelines

- The funky band that played a concert immediately after the game

By creating identifiable memory points for customers, an organization creates streams of buzz sources. People tell stories about their experiences to friends, family, and coworkers. The people and events described in the above list represent the experience of attending a Dallas Mavericks basketball game in January 2002. Mark Cuban says his chief objective for fans is a fun and memorable experience, not just a basketball game.

In *The Experience Economy,* authors Joseph Pine and James Gilmore explain how businesses that orchestrate customer experiences "open up possibilities for extraordinary economic expansion." Companies can avoid the commoditization of their products and services by creating value through memorable experiences. "Every business is a stage, and therefore work is theater," they write.[9] A customer experience can be a creative stage for performance, like Build-A-Bear

Workshop's assembly line where customers make their own teddy bears and stuffed animals. But often experiences are created just by interactions with company employees. "In the experience economy, any work observed directly by a customer must be recognized as an act of theater," the authors say.[10]

Our case-study companies understand this principle and focus on hiring memorable people. For instance, all Build-A-Bear employees attend "Bear University," a three-week training course. They learn the "Way of the Bear" and are encouraged to be imaginative and tireless in creating memorable experiences with customers. Or take our traveling experience from Baltimore one hot day in the summer of 2006 to Chicago. The air conditioning in the Baltimore airport terminal had conked out. It was hot and miserable. But that hardly bothered Mathew the Southwest gate agent. He wore a funny balloon hat on his head, told jokes to the waiting group, and ensured that most everyone who boarded the plane was amused by his antics. More than a few probably told their spouses or families about the funny gate agent with the wacky balloon hat. Air travel is stressful; Southwest hires people with strong empathy skills for this very reason.

It may seem that measuring an abstract concept like buzz is like counting stars in the sky: How do you count them? How can we possibly know what people are talking about in private conversations? But with conversations among friends and coworkers increasingly taking place in the digital world of e-mail and Web sites, patterns can be observed and measured. In her *Harvard Business Review* article, Dye says that organizations plugged into buzz networks "can predict the spread of buzz by analyzing how different groups of customers interact and influence one another."[11]

One of the largest Web sites in the world is Yahoo, the portal and search engine. It quantifies interest among its 500 million monthly visitors using a "Buzz Index." (See Figure 5.2.) Every day, Yahoo lists the most popular search terms entered into its search engine. It ranks search subjects with a "buzz score," or the percentage of users searching for a subject on a given day. (The number of searches is multiplied by a constant to make the number easier to read.) For example, on March 23, 2002, pop star Britney Spears held the number one spot with a buzz score of 166, having been on the chart for 283 days in a row. The Internal Revenue Service was number nine on Yahoo's Buzz Index—understandable, given that April 15 was three weeks away. Most entries on the hit list are famous people, which underscores the idea that people are fascinated with, and love to talk about, other people.

Yahoo is extending its buzz chart idea into a service, working with movie companies to correlate online buzz with real ticket purchases. The company tracks the number of search requests for a specific movie title during a movie's release and compares it with actual ticket sales. What they've found: A near-identical correlation between the numbers of search requests and a film's box office receipts. Yahoo has extended this buzz measurement program to other industries: finance, music, car sales. When it adds U.S. census data to the mix, a company can obtain a much clearer picture of who is talking about them, in effect seeing a clearer picture of its prospective customers.

A key to making online buzz work is proper structure, a clearly defined message, and call to action. In the Internet universe, where the underlying premise is "more is more," Yahoo's research shows that small and compact is better than big and expansive for generating new buzz, especially for entertainment products.

"Twenty-seven percent of all people who visit a Web site either watch the video or listen to the audio, which is a very concentrated short message that gets the message across," according to Tim Sanders, who was at one time the company's chief solutions officer.[12] Carefully choosing the right words that are easy to remember and repeat is important. For creating structured buzz, Sanders suggests a "ten-minute Web site." A Web site visitor knows everything she needs to know in ten minutes and can repeat several key messages easily to other people. Most important, the site asks for her e-mail

Figure 5.2 | Buzz and Box Office Results

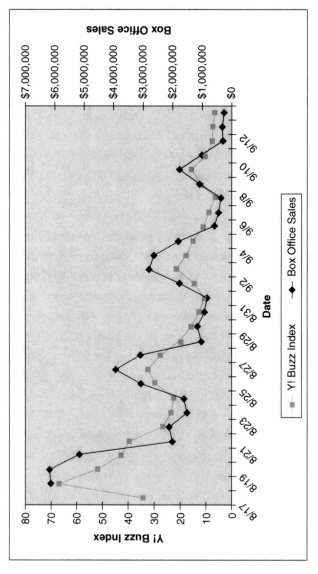

Yahoo! measures buzz as the number of times a person, place, or thing is used as a search term on its site. The company finds that the number of times a specific movie is searched for on its site often correlates with the movie's box office receipts.

Source: Yahoo! Reprinted with permission of Yahoo! Inc. © 2002 by Yahoo! Inc. YAHOO! and the YAHOO! logo are trademarks of YAHOO! Inc.

address, which encourages repeating the key messages or unlocks the door to future content.

Technorati.com is a blog search engine. It tracks millions of blogs and highlights the most frequently used search keywords and most blogged about people, books, movies, Internet videos, and news stories. Type your name, your product, or your company name into the search field to discover who's discussing you in the blogosphere. Technorati also makes it possible to create a "Watchlist" that alerts you any time the keyword you want to "watch" is mentioned on a blog.

Besides using the free tools available from technorati, here are some ideas about how to measure buzz-generation programs:

- Always ask new and prospective customers how they discovered you. Ask for the specific place, press mention, or person. If the discovery was through a personal referral, what did the referrer say?

- Add a "How did you hear about us?" question to all of your direct marketing activities, such as the sign-up form for your e-mail newsletter or print response cards. If your organization has a call center, have your reps end their calls with this line if the data is not already entered into your customer relationship management system.

- Search the Internet for places where you or your company's name is mentioned.

- Analyze traffic to your Web site. Know which organizations are visiting the most, which part of the world they're in, and which parts of the site they visit most. Most Web site traffic analysis tools can measure search terms entered into search engines that drove visitors to your site.

One way to think about this is with a meme, a self-explanatory concept that moves through a population like a virus. The word meme was coined in 1976 by Oxford biologist Richard Dawkins in his book *The Selfish Gene.* Memes communicate a complete idea simply and compactly. All of its instructions for replication are self-evident and simple.

"Examples of memes are tunes, ideas, catch-phrases, clothes fashions, ways of making pots or of building arches," Dawkins writes. "Just as genes propagate themselves in the gene pool by leaping from body to body via sperms or eggs, so memes propagate themselves in the meme pool by leaping from brain to brain via a process which, in the broad sense, can be called imitation."[13] Because it helps people understand what you offer, a meme is more than a tagline. A meme for your company's products and services helps customer evangelists tell your story more succinctly. With a few words neatly arranged in a phrase that rolls off the tongue, a meme will be transmitted from person to person like a handshake.

Which is easier to remember: "We are a marketing consulting firm that helps clients grow their businesses by getting customers to not just buy their products but believe in them so much that they tell everyone they know about them," or "Creating customer evangelists"?

There's no magic formula for creating a meme. It takes a few iterations to get it right.

It requires you to understand the value that customers say that your product or company provides. Once they experience it, your best customers can probably articulate the value of your products and services better than anyone. Ask your customers to describe in their own words how your products help them. Keep memes to a few words. The simpler it is, the easier it is to spread. First try it out on plenty of people at as many events as possible. When introducing your meme, look for signs of comprehension or confusion. Listen to how people respond. If they say, "That's just what we need. I should introduce you to our CEO," then your meme probably works. If the response is, "I'm not sure what you mean," your meme needs work.

CHAPTER SIX

Create Community

*You are cordially invited to attend our annual reunion to be held
in the Royal York Hotel in downtown Toronto. The gala event
will include dinner, entertainment, camaraderie,
and an examination of your hernia repair.*

—From an invitation to Shouldice Hospital's annual hernia patient reunion

Each year, a tightly knit group of patients from Shouldice Hospital in Thornhill, Ontario, Canada, get together and party. They have dinner, entertainment, dancing. Maybe some hula. It's a fun night. Many partygoers have two things in common: They've had hernia surgery, and they are former patients of Shouldice. It's not your ordinary hospital. It encourages patients to meet one another and build relationships. Its approach to hospitalization is that it should be an experience—a happy and memorable one, not a frightening and forgettable one. It all began in 1947 when several of Dr. Edward Earle Shouldice's patients suggested that he host a get-together for himself and his patients as a chance to renew friendships and stay in touch. Dr. Shouldice loved the idea, seeing it as the perfect opportunity to launch his idea for annual checkups and for building research data. The first party in 1948 drew 100 patients; since then, the hospital has sponsored annual reunions, with attendance topping 1,500 in the late 1980s, although the reunion has recently been pared back to just under 1,000. A committee of former patients helps the hospital plan the parties.

Shouldice Hospital looks more like a posh country club than a medical facility with its 20 acres of landscaped grounds, a solarium, and a putting green. From the outside, one might not know that inside, 7,500 hernia operations are performed each year; that's more than 30 procedures every day.

The hospital reports a 99 percent success rate with hernia repairs since 1945. It knows because it has painstakingly followed up with every patient—270,000 in all. The hospital contacts 130,000 patients every year by inviting them to the hospital for checkups, hosting the annual reunion of Shouldice alumni where an examination is included, setting up traveling clinics in small towns around Ontario for those who can't travel to the hospital, and mailing or e-mailing every single patient a follow-up survey. As Dr. Shouldice envisioned it, the hospital has created a continuous research project that enables it to understand its success rate. It also provides an opportunity to market the success rate.

But hospital officials say it's more than surgical success that lands new patients. Daryl Urquhart, the hospital's marketing director, says Shouldice focuses on creating patient communities. He says that getting to know other people leads to memorable experiences. Hospital stays last three to four days. Instead of hectic in-and-out outpatient surgery, patients are encouraged to meet other patients, resulting in a type of "empathetic therapy," an instant support group that compares notes, discusses concerns, and alleviates anxieties about common conditions. Each room has two beds so that each patient has a "buddy" during his stay. Phones and television sets are located only in communal areas; none are in patient rooms. This small detail helps keep patients out of their beds, walking around, and meeting others. Patients eat in a common dining room with tables of six. The hospital has billiards, shuffleboard, and a common area for playing cards in addition to the solarium and putting green, all of it designed to get patients meeting and talking with other patients.

During its 55-year history, Shouldice has often been the talk of Canada's medical establishment. In 2001, a study by Concordia University in Montreal found that of new patients 49 percent were referrals from former patients while 34 percent were referrals by health care professionals (physicians, chiropractors, dentists, etc.). Half of all patients heard about Shouldice from former patients, which is a rather remarkable figure. Urquhart calls those patients "the apostles." "It's our job to make sure that every patient who walks out the door is an apostle and not a terrorist," he says.[1] A terrorist, he explains, is "an unhappy customer who makes it his business to destroy your business." Urquhart says the hospital has a high rate of evangelism because "we focus on not just the surgery but on the entire experience." Much of the experience is a result of the community building among patients and the lifetime follow-up.

Organizations like Shouldice that create customer evangelists often create some form of customer community. The communities create a sense of belonging for customers, of being part of something bigger than themselves. Enabling customers to connect with each other and with you provides benefits for all the involved parties. It helps customers get advice on buying things and support for things they've already bought, as well as connect with like-minded people for social reasons. For companies, customer communities build loyalty, provide valuable feedback, and contribute to increased sales. Marketers in our case-study companies (chapters 9–14) know this to be true, although they admit the community effect can be hard to measure. For e-commerce Web sites, measuring the effect of online community is easier. A McKinsey-Jupiter Media Metrix study released in 2001 showed that users of Web community features generated two-thirds of sales despite accounting for only one-third of the site's visitors. Users who contributed product reviews or posted messages visited the Web sites nine times more often and remained twice as loyal, buying products nearly twice as often. Users who read but didn't contribute to community interaction were more frequent visitors and buyers.

Creating community has been the principle marketing strategy for Maker's Mark bourbon for most of the product's history, since Bill Samuels Sr. founded the company in 1958. Samuels never liked advertising and thought it was rude. "Being a craftsman and a southern gentleman, he abhorred the idea of getting in people's faces," says his son, Bill Samuels Jr. "Our initial marketing strategy was to sit and wait to be discovered."[2] When the company first started out, its community of customers was small enough that they knew most of them by name. As the company grew and Bill eventually took over, they were unable to stay in personal contact with their thousands of customers. "It started to bother me that we were not going to be able to have the same personal relationship with our friend and recommenders that we had had in Kentucky," Samuels told us. "How do we help get people to want to talk to us and take the initiative so we can talk back to them?"[3]

Bill Jr. came up with an idea he called the Maker's Mark Ambassadors. It's a club for the bourbon's most passionate customers. Ambassadors can sign up via the Maker's Mark Web site, and several hundred thousand have. At the site, Ambassdors can download personalized Maker's Mark business cards to distribute. Their free membership entitles them to have their names engraved on a barrel of bourbon that ages for six years. They receive regular updates from Bill Jr., who writes his folksy notes himself. Ambassadors are invited to local Marker's Mark events in their city as well as the annual Ambassador Reunion in Loretto, Kentucky. That usually attracts about 3,000 attendees from the U.S. and around the world. The reunion weekend includes horse races, a raucous party, and a tour of the historic distillery with a chance to dip bottles into red wax, the iconic feature of Maker's Mark bottles.

"We enjoy talking to our customers one-to-one," Bill Jr. says. "It is really part of our nature. And we never worry about the fact that, oh my gosh, we are only talking to 50 or 60 or 100 or 10,000 instead of a million, which you do when you try to slap everybody on the ass with an advertising message. We know that our next customers are going to come from their efforts, not our efforts."[4]

Community works differently for each organization. What's consistently the same, however, is interacting with customers to understand their connection with you and others like themselves. To bring customers together, companies use in-person events as well as online communities. In fact, combining both methods often maximizes interaction among an organization's various constituencies.

The online auction company eBay hosts some 15,000 customers every year at an event called eBay Live. Buyers, sellers, exhibitors, and anyone who wants to learn more about eBay comes from all over the world to share in the community, inspiration, and education this once-a-year event offers. Attendees meet and learn from peers who have similar interests on eBay. The three-day event features more than 150 education sessions for all levels of eBay members from newbies to Power Sellers.[5] CEO Meg Whitman and President Bill Cobb speak and pose for pictures with attendees. Customers are made to feel like celebrities as they enter the closing-night gala on a red carpet, high-fiving 700 eBay employees. Just as if they're being introduced at a big football game, a giant video screen shows customers running the gauntlet.[6]

Nestlé-owned Buitoni pasta company wants to be more than a pasta maker—it wants to be the authority on Italian food. So it created the "Casa Buitoni Club" as a customer community strategy to build loyalty. Its grassroots work with in-store sampling and sponsorship of sporting events helped Nestlé build a database of 200,000 customers in two years. These customers were invited to join the club, whose members receive recipes, a toll-free number for cooking advice, a chance to win a visit to the original Casa Buitoni villa in Tuscany, gourmet cooking weekends and plenty of opportunities to sample new products. Club membership is driven by word of mouth and notices on pasta packages. Nestlé says Buitoni pasta consumption and customer loyalty are "noticeably higher" since the club's inception.[7]

Harley-Davidson established the Harley Owners Groups (HOGs) in 1983 as a response to customers' requests for organized ways to share their passion for ownership. After two years, 49 local chapters had formed with a total membership of 60,000. By 2006, more than one million people were in HOGs covering 1,200 chapters worldwide. An April 2001 *Forbes* article described the passion that Harley-Davidson customers feel about the company as something akin to a "movement that existed before you were born and will continue beyond your finite life span."[8]

Communities can meet regularly online, too: Nancy White, president of Full Circle Consulting, created the Online Facilitation e-mail group in August 1999. She leads the group with its several thousand members through discussions of the best practices of online facilitation as well as sharing resources and ideas. White indirectly markets her experience every day by leading and moderating the forum.[9]

Weekly or monthly e-mail newsletters help organizations share their latest knowledge of specific topics. O'Reilly Media, the technical book publisher, produces several dozen newsletters and blogs that cover topics from Linux and Java to Perl. There are even special newsletters for librarians, professors, and book retailers. The informative and well-written newsletters deliver real value. Each newsletter has a different editor at the company who includes such information as "Tips for Building Web Database Applications." The O'Reilly model delivers a newsletter of value for a community of subscribers, not one that mindlessly hypes products.

Are there fan sites or blogs for your product or service? Embrace them! Extol them for the heroes they are. Consider linking to the best ones. Give Web-based fans special access to pictures and information they can use to build their sites. Send them gift certificates, invitations to special events . . . anything to recognize them for their evangelism. The worst strategy to deal with genuine fan sites: sending cease and desist letters. In late 2000, Warner Brothers sent letters to hundreds of Harry Potter fan sites, insisting they were infringing on the company's intellectual property rights. The media giant told the teenage Webmasters to take their sites down and, in some cases, demanded they transfer ownership of domain names, such as *HarryPotter-world.com,* to Warner Brothers. One angry 15-year-old British fan, Claire Field, took her story to the press, and within days the story made headlines across the country. Two different activist organizations were formed to protest the legal action: PotterWar and Defense Against the Dark Arts (DADA). DADA organized a boycott of all Harry Potter paraphernalia.[10] Companies that send "nastygrams" to fans who build shrines to a company's products and services are themselves nasty.

Instead, recruit fan sites to help you with marketing. Gordon Paddison, senior vice president of worldwide interactive marketing for New Line Cinema, is responsible for the official *Lord of the Rings* movie Web site. Before building it, he contacted the Webmasters of over 400 fan sites dedicated to J. R. R. Tolkien's literary trilogy.

"I wanted to establish a relationship early on with the influencers, people that I felt would be a conduit for information," Paddison said.[11] The resulting site was filled with screen savers, desktop images, hundreds of still photos, and interviews with the cast and crew. The Paddison strategy is to partner with fan sites and feed them insider tips, thereby inducing them to recruit passionate followers who spread the movie's message.

General Motors, Southwest Airlines, Microsoft, and other small businesses alike use blogs to connect with their customer community. Southwest has used its blog to gather feedback from customers to consider changing its no-assigned seat policy. Southwest president Colleen Barrett uses the company blog to update customers on changes to the Wright Amendment, a federal law that prohibits the airline from flying from Dallas directly to states that are not directly next to Texas.

Widening the company's lobbying efforts to the company's blog may have helped their cause: Congress repealed the Wright Amendment with a compromise reached during a late night in September

2006. The ban of flights will be totally lifted by 2014, but Southwest was able to start booking passengers out of Love Field through to cities in states not directly connected to Texas. Southwest's strategy was that the more people in its community of customers knew about the protectionist nature of the Wright Amendment, the better. That plan seemed to have worked.

Creating community requires a personal touch. Customers want to know about features, functions, or methodologies of products and services; feature comparisons and product descriptions are a key part of any firm's sales efforts. But prospective customers also want to know about the people side of the equation: Who else has purchased from you? Do they recommend you to others? Who are the people behind your company? Too often, Web sites, brochures, and ads feature inanimate objects, such as skylines, empty rooms, empty buildings, disconnected body parts, sunsets, sunrises, clocks, watches, glasses, flocks of geese, unintelligible artistic pieces, or just about anything except real-life people. It's as if the people have been snatched away.

A customer community helps prospects identify with and connect with other people. People are the ideal focus for marketing efforts, especially customers. Chances are that the front page of your Web site is your most visited page, so it's an excellent spot to feature customers. Your featured customers are likely to tell friends and colleagues about their stardom on your site. How easy is it to contact the people at your organization? Is everyone invisible or do you humanize your company by making some form of communication with them possible? Is there a forum for your customers to meet and if so, do your company executives make appearances in the forum or at least read what's being written? Too often senior managers are able to hide from the world and end up being shielded from the opinions of customers and prospects. A key lesson from our case-story companies is that key leaders make themselves accessible to a wide array of customers.

Do your business cards have a face? If you're a heavy-duty networker or salesperson, you probably meet dozens of people every month, perhaps every week. Those prospects have a better chance of remembering you when you follow up if they can put a face to a name. Try putting your picture on your business card. It's not just for real estate agents anymore. Feature portraits and bios of your company people on your Web site. Let prospects see the personalities behind the corporate curtain. Photos of stern expressions communicate that your company is unfriendly. Smile—it's a portrait, not a police mug shot. Candid photography is better. Develop customer case studies. Prove how your company has solved customer problems. Feature quotations from customers, not from your project managers. Then brag about the case studies anywhere and everywhere. Make them a central tool of your salesforce. Humanize your company's e-mail correspondence. Adopt a more casual conversational style of writing. Correspondence should come from a real person, not "The Management." Avoid the dreaded "Please do not reply to this e-mail" notation. Instead of trying to modify what is a natural inclination, try modifying your own system.

People are loyal to people, not necessarily brands. If you humanize your marketing, you're on the road to creating customer evangelists. Creating community is key to creating customer evangelists. Community encourages customers to bond with one another underneath the umbrella of your organization's goodwill. One of the strategies to introduce new customers to your community is to offer a specialized, smaller offering, or what we call a "bite-size chunk."

CHAPTER SEVEN

Bite-Size Chunks

Nothing is particularly hard if you divide it into small jobs.[1]

—Henry Ford

Every day, entrepreneurs or sales managers sit down at their desk and ask themselves, "How do I get more people to know about us?" Obscurity is their primary problem. Some companies spend lavishly to fight pervasive obscurity, while others outmaneuver competitors to build recognition and buzz without spending a small fortune to annoy the world about their presence.

One cause of obscurity, especially the chronic variety, is not enough word of mouth. A company or product may live too deep in the shadows where not enough people see it. Or it may live among other popular products but it's being ignored or picked over in favor of others. Why? Customers say your company produces a solid, reputable product and delivers personable, honest service, so why are you getting beat? Why aren't you the cool kid on the block? One answer may be that not enough people, or not enough of the right people, have tried your product or service. There isn't enough buzz to get the cool people talking or blogging about you. Another answer may be that your product or service is expensive and for them to experience it, they have to buy it. If either one of those answers is the case, it's time to consider the bite-size chunk strategy. Entice prospects with a taste of what's to come. If they bite, they'll probably buy more. The sampling world has understood this well for years. The advantage for the company new to sampling is that buzz about it can spread quickly. Trial products, trial subscriptions, or all manner of samples can be fast and affordable word-of-mouth marketing campaigns that can lead to new ranks of evangelists. Breaking product and service portfolios into bite-size chunks makes your company more accessible, too. For some products, it's samples. For other products, a limited-time or limited-capacity trial version works well. For others, it's a public workshop that provides a service. A "starter" product or service lets customers try your lower-end offerings on their way to purchasing your high-end, more expensive, and complex products.

Breaking your product into bite-size chunks helps create customer evangelists because it reduces the risk for first-time purchasers. It eliminates inhibitors to the purchase, such as cost or time, and goes far to fighting obscurity. Samples or trials get your product into customers' hands and minds. It shortens the sales cycle and provides a strategic opportunity for customers to experience your products sooner rather than later. It builds goodwill with customers because it provides value without requiring a purchase, no matter the level of investment. That's a key item: bite-size chunks provide up-front value. Give to receive. By extending an offer of trust, you implicitly tell customers that you are trustworthy. You're genuine. You are easy to work with. Not everyone will buy, certainly, but your product isn't for everyone at every moment in their life. Don't let the potential for a tiny percentage of customers taking advantage of your goodwill stop you from offering a bite-size chunk. It's the benefit of reaching all of the other desirable customers you're seeking who, if they are inspired enough, may spread the word.

Sampling works well for inexpensive products. Consumer packaged goods companies, like P&G and Unilever, have used this technique for decades by mailing free samples of laundry detergent and shampoo to homes. If you have a great product, half the battle is just getting the customer to try it. Sampling provides the lowest barrier to entry in trying a product. After all, most of us can't resist an offer to try something new and free. A January 2001 survey by Brand Marketing and the Promotion Marketing Association found that sampling is highly effective for marketers of consumer packaged goods. It asked 1,195 people about their bite-size chunk habits and found that:

• 95 percent have tried a sample.

• 38 percent have tried every sample they have received in the past year.

• 92 percent decided to buy a grocery, household, or health and beauty care product after trying a sample.

• 73 percent became aware of new or improved products through samples.

• 84 percent would consider switching products if they liked the free sample.[2]

The technology industry has had tremendous success using bite-size chunks for creating starter evangelists. Many consumer software companies let prospective customers try a product for a limited time. Customers download free a full-featured version of the software from the company's Web site before it expires after 30 to 90 days or a limited number of uses.

Here's how our case-study companies have employed bite-size chunk strategies:

• SolutionPeople—This creativity consulting firm for the Fortune 500 charges $60,000 for several days of creative brainstorming, but prospective customers can send a representative to a daylong public session for $850. They typically enjoy a 50 to 65 percent conversion process for prospects to engage the company for the several-day project.[3]

- Dallas Mavericks—What's it like to be a season ticket holder for this NBA team? Fans can find out by buying five-game and ten-game packets of tickets. If they like their seats and the overall experience, they can upgrade to a half-season or full-season membership. The team's marketing chief says 55 percent of customers upgrade.[4]

- IBM—Its "Test Drive" program lets programmers test Linux applications online in a simulated IBM environment without having to actually buy IBM hardware.

- Build-A-Bear Workshop—Kids can have their birthday parties at the stores. Partygoers who are new to the store sample the experience of building their first bear.

Figure 7.1 illustrates how different companies create bite-size chunks of their products and services.

As Henry Ford once said, "Nothing is particularly hard if you divide it into small jobs." By dividing your product and service into discrete pieces, you increase exponentially the likelihood of building buzz that leads to creating new customer evangelists.

Now that customers have tried your product, do they believe in it? Does buying your product contribute to a greater good? Customers believe in causes important to them, and they want to contribute to the success of those causes; if buying your product supports a popular and highly thought of cause, then you are on your way to new levels of loyalty.

Figure 7.1 | A Sampling of Companies' Bite-Size Chunks

Company	Premium Offering / Price	Bite-Size Chunk/Price
Harley-Davison	Motorcycle / $6,000–16,000 retail	Rent a Harley to ride for a day / $120
WebTrendsLive	Software that monitors Web site usage / $35 to $2,000 per month	Limited-use version / free
SolutionPeople	Creativity and innovation training / $60,000 for 3 days	KnowBrainer tool / $75
Faith Popcorn	Keynote speeches / $25,000	Book / $25 retail

CHAPTER EIGHT

Create a Cause

Evangelism is the process of selling a dream.[1]

—Guy Kawasaki

Guy Kawasaki and his compatriots at Apple Computer borrowed religion-based evangelism and took it to work. Apple's secular evangelism launched a new computer that suffered from insufficient software, a lack of storage capacity, a small screen, and a price point higher than its competition. Yet the Mac could compete with lower-priced, richer-featured models made by IBM because Apple was selling a dream, not a computer. Apple focused on the promise of what the Macintosh could deliver, which was to improve everyone's productivity and creativity. It created an evangelism department and hired marketers to evangelize, evangelize, evangelize.

But to grow, Apple had to convince software vendors to write applications for its operating system. Kawasaki's key competitor—IBM—was a technology stalwart used to setting the standards in the industry; at one point it was even decreed a monopolist. Apple convinced a number of vendors to believe in the Macintosh cause by portraying Big Blue as Big Brother.

To build momentum for its cause, Apple ended up creating what is arguably the most famous television ad in history. Shown only once, during the 1984 Superbowl, Apple's "1984" television commercial famously portrayed Apple's unique, counterculture positioning. Directed by Ridley Scott (who also directed the films *Blade Runner* and *Alien,* among others), the ad portrayed a scowling Orwellian Big Brother figure projected on a giant screen, brainwashing a crowd of glassy-eyed sycophants. Saving the day is a female sledgehammer-thrower whose expert toss destroys the image of Big Brother, allowing everyone to see real light behind the visage. With the Macintosh, a voiceover promises that "1984 won't be like *1984,*" George Orwell's classic tale of a world in which "groupthink" is the norm and individualism outlawed. Although the company denied it at the time, Apple's ad pitted itself as David against the IBM Goliath. Nothing less than personal and global freedom was at stake. It was a powerful ad, and it put a stake in the ground.

"Macintosh started as a vision; then it became a product supported by a cult; finally, it became a cause—propagated by thousands of Macintosh evangelists," says Kawasaki.[2]

That's: vision + product + cult + cause = evangelists

Customer evangelism begins with a great product brought forth from the vision of a leader who has recognized a need in the world. The cult supports the product in its early stages. As the cult or, more appropriately, the customer community grows in size with the support of the organization, the community begins to self-organize around a cause. A good cause is meaningful; it is something to believe in and rally around. Five goals for a company's cause can include:

1. A well-defined vision

2. Making people better

3. Generating big effects

4. Catalyzing selfless actions

5. Polarizing people[3]

A vision is someone's grand plan to change the world—a piece of someone's soul. The vision of Apple founder Steve Jobs was to bring computers to the people—the free thinkers, the creative spirits. So we have just made an argument that Apple's advertising captured the imaginations of its earliest fans, setting itself apart from its competitors. Advertising is powerful, right? It can be, but the year 1984 was a different time. Cable television was in its early formation. The World Wide Web was still ten years away. The total number of mass media choices available to the typical American citizen could be counted on two hands, so naturally the Apple ad was influential. It was great theater, and it presented a vision. But the context of popular culture today and the role mass media plays in it are different, just as the mass media context will be different 20 years from now.

When something helps people change their lives, that vastly improves its chances of creating grassroots support. They tell everyone about the experience; in other words, they become evangelists. This is why self-help books are often best-sellers; sales are fueled by word of mouth of how a book helped change someone's life. Causes can create profound change and affect vast numbers of people. A habitual drunk driver killed Candy Lightner's 13-year-old daughter in 1980. He pleaded guilty but served no jail time and ten months later, he could legally drive again. An outraged Lightner launched Mothers Against Drunk Driving (MADD). In 2002, MADD's two million members in 600 chapters blanketed all 50 states, resulting in considerably tougher drunk-driving laws. Lightner's cause thus had big effects. Catalyzing, or inspiring, selfless actions is best explained as doing business by the Golden Rule: just do the right thing. For example, after 9/11, tens of thousands of airline workers were furloughed or idled. The majority of skycaps' earnings come from tips. During the shutdown of U.S. air travel, Southwest Airlines elected to pay the skycaps what they would have otherwise made, a notably selfless action. For Southwest, it was simply a decision of doing the right thing. No one gets rich working as a skycap, and Southwest pitched in to help out a segment of colleagues in need.

Causes have the power to change society. When we think of organizations with causes, we usually think of such nonprofits as the Susan G. Komen Breast Cancer Foundation or the Salvation Army. The cause is the organization's reason for being. Its members wear their values on their sleeves, often literally. People who feel strongly about an issue naturally seek alliances with others who feel the same. Coauthors Richard Cross and Janet Smith outline how "identity bonds" are formed between customer and company. "Identity bonds are formed when customers admire and identify with values, attitudes, or lifestyle preferences that they associate with your brand or product," they write in *Customer Bonding: 5 Steps to Lasting Customer Loyalty.* "Customers form an emotional attachment based on their perception of those shared values."[4]

Emotional attachment is key to creating customer evangelists. The two simple ways to build emotional attachment are to (1) adopt a charitable cause (often called cause-related marketing or social-cause marketing) and (2) sell dreams instead of products. Let's look at the differences between these two concepts.

Adopting a Charitable Cause

In 1983, American Express launched a three-month campaign to support refurbishment of the Statue of Liberty. The company donated one cent every time a customer used an American Express card and one dollar for every new account. The program raised $1.7 million for restoration, and overall American Express card usage rose 28 percent during the campaign's first month; new card applications increased 45 percent.[5] American Express is credited with coining the term *cause-related marketing.* Business in the Community, a London-based organization focused on corporate social responsibility, defines the term as "a commercial activity by which businesses and charities form a partnership with each other to market an image, product, or service for mutual benefit."[6] Since the advent of American Express's successful campaign, companies have increasingly embraced cause-related marketing. According to the International Events Group, business investing in cause programs jumped more than 400 percent from $125 million in 1990 to $545 million in 1998.

Now more than a short-term tactic to spike sales, cause-related marketing has evolved into a positioning discipline to enhance corporate images with significant bottom-line and community aspects, says Carol Cone, Chairman of Cone, Inc., a strategic marketing firm that develops and implements cause programs.[7] Her research in the Cone/Roper Cause Related Trends Report has found that American consumers consistently support cause-related programs. The 1999 report found that given a buying choice between two products of equivalent price and quality:

- 78 percent of adults said they'd be more likely to buy a product associated with a cause they care about.

- 66 percent said they'd switch brands to support a cause.

- 61 percent said they'd switch retailers to support a cause.

- 54 percent would pay more for a product that supported a cause they care about.

The Cone/Roper survey found that 80 percent of Americans prefer companies that commit to a specific cause for a long period over those that opt for multiple, short-period causes. Cone calls the former companies "cause branders," that is, companies that take a long-term, stake holder–based approach to integrating social issues into business strategy, brand equity, and organizational identity.[8] Companies that support causes for the long haul win the hearts of customers.

Figure 8.1 outlines companies and their highly visible cause-related marketing efforts.

In a world of so much stuff, how do you make your product stand out? Sell something bigger than the product itself. Sell a dream. Attract customers by demonstrating that you are in the game for more than meeting your quarterly sales numbers. Evangelize how you are helping your customers live better lives.

This doesn't mean slapping a dreamy slogan on a product and announcing that it will change your customer's life forever. Plenty of late-night TV infomercials already make that dubious promise, and customers are skeptical of contrived playacting marketing. Marrying a product to a cause is not something the marketing department dreams up. A cause helps customers and, most important, embodies the principles and values of an organization's leaders and employees. From the receptionist to the CEO, all company employees show that they believe in the cause with their actions every day. The marketing department communicates the cause's message on the Web, in brochures, through its PR, and in advertising. Figure 8.2 outlines companies selling more than just products.

Figure 8.1 | A Sampling of Companies' Cause-Related Marketing

Company	Products	Cause(s)
Ben & Jerry's	Ice cream	Support and encourage organizations to eliminate underlying causes of environmental and social problems
The Body Shop	Cosmetics, toiletries	Environmentalism, human rights
Whole Foods	Natural and organic foods	Global organic farming; local food banks; 5 percent of total net profits go to not-for-profit organizations
Wal-Mart	General merchandise	Environment, children, education, community
Avon	Beauty products, jewelry	Women's health, including breast cancer awareness

Source: Company Web sites

The idea of cause-driven companies cannot be underestimated, no matter the product. Let's take two well-known companies and explore how they could rally customers around a cause. (Note: these are suggestions for causes, not actual programs they have undertaken.) The two companies are Coca-Cola, maker of one of the best-known products in the world, and Oral B, a manufacturer of toothbrushes and other dental products. We then asked two well-known and respected cause-creation experts how the unlikeliest candidates for a company cause—consumer products—could build support for their products. Our experts were: Dan Pallotta, an entrepreneur who founded Pallotta TeamWorks, a charitable event-marketing firm based in Los Angeles; and Brian Erwin, publisher of Crestport Press, which publishes books on heath, healing, and personal growth. Erwin is also the former head of marketing for O'Reilly & Associates and the former director of activism for the Sierra Club.

Figure 8.2 | A Sampling of Companies That Sell More Than Products

Company	Products	Cause(s)
Apple	Macintosh personal computer	The "democratization of the desktop," whereby previously expensive and exclusive programs and processes are affordable and easier to use
Southwest Airlines	Air transportation	Freedom to connect with loved ones (because of consistently lower airfares)
Starbucks	Coffee	A meeting point for neighborhoods and communities
Dallas Mavericks	Professional basketball	Creating emotional memories
Fast Company	Magazine subscriptions	Showcases the companies and individuals who are inventing the future and reinventing business

How can Coke create a cause? Dan Pallotta says Coca-Cola should "do something really, really radical" if it wants to differentiate itself from Pepsi. "They've got what, $700 million in advertising dollars this year? Here's what we're going to recommend: spend the whole $700 million on a campaign about recycling your Coke cans. Don't talk about the flavor; you got that. People love you. Now make a difference in the world and people will really love you."[9]

How can Oral B, the toothbrush maker, create a cause? Brian Erwin says it's tough but possible. "Maybe I'm not loyal to the toothbrush itself, even though it's a fine toothbrush. But a good corporate entity that does good things in the world will engineer my loyalty, and that will have a positive impact on its brand. If given the choice in the drugstore, I would be inclined to pick that brand. There is an important element of how a company acts as a corporate entity."[10]

Creating a cause is easy. Getting people to join your cause is hard. Television ads are broadcast. Brochures are delivered. The Web site is up. Customers discover your company, your product, and your cause, and they want more information. They are considering joining your cause. Now is the moment of truth. Can people actually join your cause? A simple question, but it can be a serious problem if you can't capitalize on the interest and excitement you've generated. Customers will get frustrated and lose interest if the process isn't smooth. In *Selling the Dream,* Kawasaki illustrated the complexities of joining a cause. As an experiment in July 1990, his researcher called eight organizations to inquire about signing up.

The researcher called Apple, NeXT, and IBM and asked how to join their programs for developers. Then the researcher called Handgun Control, Inc. and the National Rifle Association and asked for information on membership and volunteer opportunities. Finally, the researcher called the National Audubon Society, Planned Parenthood, and the Sierra Club and asked for instructions on joining their causes.

The results were almost comical. Three out of eight organizations never sent materials and a corporate operator for one of the companies had no idea what her organization's cause was even about. How have things improved for these same organizations 12 years later? On February 17, 2002, we decided to find out. We used the same methodology but substituted Microsoft for NeXT (which was bought and folded into Apple in December 1996). In 1990, the World Wide Web didn't exist, so Kawasaki's researcher requested information via telephone; in 2001, all of the organizations had a Web site. Certainly, after having been taken to school by Kawasaki 12 years before, these companies had made joining their causes easy, right? Not necessarily.

Apple

www.apple.com

A front-page link for "Developer" took us to the Apple Developer Connection (ADC) area, which featured information on every level of the ADC program. We clicked on the very prominent "Join now" button and signed up for the program's lowest level. Signing up online was easy, free, and painless, but the form was several pages long. Although the site promised one, we did not receive a confirmation e-mail but did begin receiving weekly ADC e-mail newsletters.

Result: Joining was easy.

IBM

www.ibm.com

IBM's front-page link for "Developers" took us to pages with bountiful amounts of information on products and technologies, but there was no information on how to join its developer program or whether a developer program existed. We signed up for something called the developerWorks e-mail newsletter. A feedback button on the page clicked through to a feedback form, and we asked how to join IBM's developer program. Two days later, an e-mail from Jeannette arrived informing us developerWorks was a content site and that we should join PartnerWorld for Developers. Jeannette included a link, which took us to a Web page to sign up as a "commercial member." After filling out and submitting a very long form, we received a confirmation e-mail in minutes.

Result: Joined, but process was confusing.

Microsoft

www.microsoft.com

A "Developer" link on the front page of its site took us to the Microsoft Developer Network (MSDN) page, but it wasn't clear how to join the program. There was lots of information on products and technologies, downloads, training, and events. We decided to just sign up for the free newsletter, but this required a Passport account, too. Four pages later, we had signed up for the Passport account. A confirmation e-mail arrived a few minutes later. We've been receiving MSDN e-mails every two weeks.

Result: Couldn't find anything but the e-mail newsletter list to join.

Handgun Control, Inc.

www.bradycampaign.org

Finding this site required research. On June 14, 2001, Handgun Control changed its name to the Brady Campaign to Prevent Gun Violence. The word *join* was nowhere on the front page of the site, but a button for "Activists" took us to a page that encouraged us to "Become an Activist." We were then presented with the following choices:

- Join the B.E.A.R.

- Write your member of Congress.

- Write to your local newspaper.

- Start Campus Alliance at your school.

- Join the Hechinger Speakers Bureau.

- Give online.

Not knowing what "B.E.A.R" was, it seemed that "join" would take us in the right direction. Clicking the button took us to the "Brady E-Action Response Network." After filling out and submitting the online form, we got an error page.

Note: We gave the Brady Campaign another try a few months later. After completing and submitting the online form, we received a confirmation e-mail in minutes. The Web site's navigation was slightly improved.

Result: Couldn't join on the first try. Successful on second attempt.

National Rifle Association (NRA)

www.nra.org

A button called "Join/Renew" on the site's front page took us to another page, where we had to click again on "Join NRA." Very little information could be found on the benefits of membership except that $3.75 of membership dues is designated for a subscription to the organization's magazine. We filled out the form, including our credit card information for the $10 fee. A confirmation e-mail arrived in minutes.

Result: Joined, but unsure of the benefits.

National Audubon Society

www.audubon.org

A button called "Join & Support" on the site's front page took us to a page that clearly explained membership benefits. We clicked on the "Join now" button but received an error page.

Note: We tried the National Audubon Society a few months later. This time we were able to fill out the membership form and join at a cost of $20. No confirmation e-mail was received.

Result: Couldn't join at first. Successful on second attempt.

Planned Parenthood

www.plannedparenthood.org

A button called "Get Involved" on the front page of the Web site took us to a very busy page that listed many of the following actions to take next:

- Speak out to save *Roe v. Wade.*

- Send a Message of Thanks to Colin Powell for His Support of Condom Use.

- Sign the Petition for Choice!

- Sign the Petition Opposing the Nomination of Judge Pickering.

- Don't De-fund International Family Planning.

- Don't Relegate Women to a Second-Class Status!

- Demand Funding for Comprehensive Sexuality Education.

- Support Contraceptive Equity Legislation.

It was unclear how to simply join Planned Parenthood's cause. A button invited us to join the "Responsible Choices Action Network" from where we could send e-mails and faxes to every member of Congress on issues relating to family planning, sexuality education, and reproductive health. The network, according to the site, would send us e-mail regarding legislation and how to take action. After submitting a form to register for the Responsible Choices Action Network, we did not receive a confirmation e-mail. Several days later, however, the action network sent an e-mail urging us to oppose the nomination of Charles F. Pickering Sr. to the U.S. Court of Appeals for the Fifth Circuit by replying to the e-mail. (We didn't.) We've been receiving about two e-mails every week since we signed up.

Result: Not sure if we joined Planned Parenthood or just an e-mail list.

Sierra Club

www.sierraclub.org

A button called "Join or Give" on the site's front page took us to a page with detailed explanations of membership benefits, including how membership money is used. We clicked the "Join online now" button, filled out the form with our credit card information, and received a confirmation page. It cost $25 to join at the lowest level, but we did not receive an e-mail confirmation of our transaction. We received *Sierra* magazine two weeks later and a Sierra Club backpack a few weeks after that.

Result: Easy to join.

The World Wide Web has certainly improved the ability to get information quickly. Because each organization had a Web site, we could obtain more than what Kawasaki's researcher could 12 years earlier. Actually joining the causes was sometimes complex and a few times impossible. Technology is only great when it works. Rallying supporters to join your cause is like dating: once they're ready to commit, don't jilt them at the altar.

Besides an embrace of customer evangelism tenets, we found these additional corollaries.

- A visible leader. The willingness of the company founder, chief executive, or senior leader to be out there was key. It often means someone who speaks his mind and does not duck from controversy within his industry. Note: This is different than the charismatic CEO who leads totally by personality rather than leading by example. Employees and customers want company presidents to be accessible.

- A recurring insistence on "doing the right thing." This consistently applies to customers, employees, and business partners. Companies with legions of customer evangelists recognize that profit is a byproduct of evangelism, not its central purpose.

- A rather theatrical approach to business. It seems that good business means good theater. The May Department Store Company's chairman Stanley Goodman used to say, "When customers have fun, they spend more money."[11]

- An intolerance for being "cheap." This is not the same as being cost-conscious.

- A maniacal focus on customer satisfaction. We found that whereas shareholder value is important, it does not necessarily reside at the top of the company's objectives. Increasing customer value does.

CHAPTER NINE

SolutionPeople:
The High-Flying
Solutionman

Judge intelligence by the answers given to questions.
Judge creativity by the questions asked.[1]

—**Gerald Haman,** founder and president of SolutionPeople

In 1989, Gerald Haman spent $2,500 to launch his million-dollar business. Haman's company is SolutionPeople, a Chicago-based creativity, innovation, training, and consulting firm. It helps companies brainstorm ideas for new products and services, solve existing problems, and improve teamwork skills. Haman launched SolutionPeople, not long after the elder George Bush was being sworn in as president, based on the idea that training should be fun and the tools for it should be perpetually useful.

Haman bet that investing a few thousand dollars to mingle with the 5,000 attendees at the meeting of the American Society for Training and Development at the Dallas, Texas, convention center would be a good strategy for launching his company. The human resources and training professionals who make up the ASTD get together every year to discuss the latest techniques and methodologies to train people in their companies. At the convention, Haman's booth was next to that of Ned Herrmann, a well-known creativity specialist whose book *Creative Brain* had just been released. Herrmann was a biggie in the business during his career and, in Haman's eyes, a giant who could squash all upstarts. But being next to Herrmann was a good omen. An unofficial blessing.

"I've never even thought of putting myself in the same class as Herrmann because he was such a pioneer in the field," Haman says. "A lot of his research is a model for ours. His thinking influenced mine. And we were at the same conference in Dallas. That's interesting; I've never thought of that before but yes, I think it was an omen."[2]

This moment in Haman's history did not come lightly. His was a bootstrapped company and to save on expenses he recruited his sister, Elaine, to staff the convention booth with him. They took turns going to the bathroom. Haman didn't arrive at the convention totally empty-handed. He'd created a handheld tool he called the Pocket Innovator that training professionals could carry in their pocket. Like a deck of cards but with a binding, each card in the Pocket Innovator was filled with provocative questions that would spur its users to think about their problem creatively. Haman's bet paid off. Buzz about the little tool spread quickly on the trade show's floor. People lined up dozens deep to purchase the Pocket Innovator.

"I think we captured some attention for having a unique tool that people wanted to get their hands on," he notes. "If there's one theme that has allowed us to have people walk away as evangelists it is everybody gets a tool that can help them to a certain degree."[3] Because his product got people talking, Haman landed two big clients immediately: Hewlett-Packard and Digital Equipment Corporation. In the weeks later, Haman eventually signed up 50 clients from that weeklong convention in Dallas. The tool and Haman's company accomplished something that most start-ups dream about: They were instant hits. The Pocket Innovator took an ongoing need (innovation) and displayed it in a format that seemed natural but had never been used before. The tool itself became a source of evangelism.

He grossed $87,000 his first year in business. Nearly two decades later, his business had grown to occupy several studios in a converted warehouse in Chicago's West Loop. When he launched the company,

Haman had few competitors in what's loosely called the "creativi
consulting" industry. In 2002, the landscape of consultants who take
organizations through a systematic creativity process is filled with
competitors big and small, from McKinsey to Eureka Ranch and Gary
Hamel's Strategos. Haman's work has taken him all over the world,
including Singapore, where he helped 7,500 people at a stadium generate 454,000 ideas in 60 minutes. There he set three Guinness World
Records: the highest volume of ideas generated in 60 minutes; the
largest brainstorming team ever assembled; and the largest team of
facilitators ever assembled. A survey conducted by Northwestern University's Kellogg Alumni Consulting Group reported that Solution-
People has helped its clients generate over one million ideas valued
at one billion dollars. Haman keeps a framed copy of his first pay-
check—a $29,000 endorsement from Digital Equipment—in his
office. His marketing methodology from the beginning was to investigate what people needed and then to create tools and ideas to
meet those needs.

Haman has always been on the creative side of business. In the
early 1980s, he was a concert promoter for Air Supply and Cheap Trick.
Tiring of the road, he landed at Procter & Gamble in 1982, selling
Crest and Scope. He migrated to Big Five consulting firm Arthur
Andersen in 1987, where he was a researcher in the company's professional education division. It was at Andersen that Haman's ideas
for his own company started to take shape. Frustrated that few people at Andersen seemed to care much for the overweight training
manuals the company issued in bulky three-ring binders, Haman
decided to test a hypothesis: Did anyone really use the things?

"The firm was spending millions of dollars a year on training materials," he says. "The only people who seemed to appreciate them were
the people who designed them. They would go in for their performance

'eah, I developed this one-day seminar, and here's my binder. Look what I accomplished.'"[5]

g Five consulting professional he was at the time, Haman launched a formal study. His hunch that the girth of the training binders made them impractical to use consistently proved right. One day, while shopping in a tile store, Haman picked up a swatch of tile color samples, and the proverbial lightbulb—Haman's trademark icon—clicked on. How about a training tool that could fit in one's pocket yet provide structure for the creative process? With that, the Pocket Innovator tool—which eventually became the KnowBrainer tool—was born. (See Figure 9.1)

Figure 9.1 | The KnowBrainer

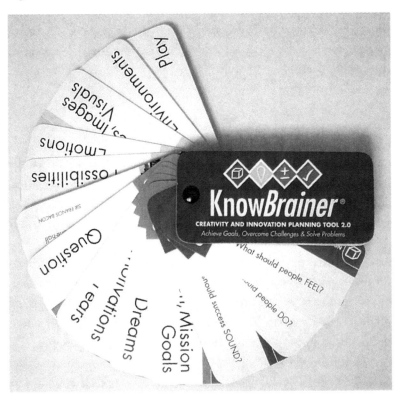

The KnowBrainer tool works much like color sample strips in a paint store. Imagine 96 of the strips bolted together with information on each side. Add scads of descriptive phrases and provocative questions such as, "What is needed, wanted, or wished?" or "What should people KNOW?" Organize them according to four strategic categories of "Investigate, Create, Evaluate, and Activate" (what Haman calls the Diamond Solution Process), and you have the KnowBrainer tool.

What makes the tool a strategic and viral element of Haman's marketing prowess? For starters, it's portable, slipping easily into a purse, a pocket, or a palm. It's unlike most other training tools, although the KnowBrainer seems familiar—just like holding those color swatches from the tile or paint store. In evangelism marketing terms, the KnowBrainer tool is a Napsterized version of Haman's knowledge. Using it day-to-day doesn't require a $150 per hour consultant (although it can help).

"My attitude has been to get as many of these out there as possible so that people talk about them," Haman says. "Napsterized is a good way to think about it. If you think about the ease of sharing, that's key, although these are difficult to photocopy, and I don't know if people would go through the work of copying one of these, which has been one of the clever aspects about it."[6]

In addition, the KnowBrainer works pretty well as a sales tool for landing future customers. Haman ships the KnowBrainer to prospects in advance of their meeting and uses it to discover the companies' problems and issues. "It always makes for an engaging discussion," Haman says.[7] Unlike most traditional marketing trinkets, this one provides real value. "What makes it viral is that it feels pretty good to have in the palm of your hand. It just feels comfortable to have around to play with. But if everyone can generate some ideas that are useful, they're going to tell other people and say, 'Hey, this helped me; it might help you.' Then I think the virality potential is really good."[8]

Haman launched SolutionPeople without four-color brochures or a Web site (it was 1989, after all) and with not much marketing collateral: just a well-defined service, a solid elevator pitch, and a contagious tool that created buzz. "We didn't even have a letterhead until about two years after we started," Haman says.[9] For those who labor under an assumption that growth comes from advertising strategies dedicated to creating brand awareness and building brand equity, Haman's success is evidence that a grassroots approach can build a long-term, sustainable company. It can even work for a company that wishes to remain small, which is Haman's objective.

"Can I imagine having built my business through advertising?" Haman asks, then laughs. "It's kind of fun to think about it, I imagine. But no, I can't."[10]

Thirteen years after SolutionPeople landed its first customer, the company still lacks four-color brochures. Other than its Web site, *www.solutionpeople.com,* the company has not produced any sales collateral. Haman has grown his business through membership in organizations, appearances at conferences and networking events, and, most significantly, referrals from friends and associates. To understand the sources of his referral base, let's begin with the personal, people-based evangelism that SolutionPeople has enjoyed. We spent a few hours with Haman in the "Thinkubator," Haman's name for his studio, to trace the routes that have led to his client engagements. Because Haman maintains a database of nearly everyone he's met, we were able to build diagrams of the connections. Using big sheets of paper we taped to the wall, we created a detailed network map of people, association memberships, and speaking engagements. Three hours later, we had scribbled names, dates, companies, and events on five separate easel sheets. We left the Thinkubator convinced that even one person can create a confluence of connections and a roster of paying clients.

Take, for instance, Dan Pink, the author of *Free Agent Nation,* a book about the growing ranks of the self-employed in the United States. At one point in his career, Pink was the chief speechwriter for Vice President Al Gore. He's also what author Emanuel Rosen calls a "network hub": a person of influence whom people rely on for information. Haman calls Pink "a master networker." In 1998, Pink posted a note to *Fast Company's* online communities, which are known as Company of Friends cells (see chapter 6). At the time, Pink was conducting research for *Free Agent Nation* and visiting groups around the country to meet free agents.

Enter Neil Kane, a friend of Haman's since the early 1990s. Kane told Haman about the online note and encouraged Haman to contact Pink. Haman did, and they enjoyed a good conversation. As a result, Pink recommended to his colleagues at *Fast Company* that SolutionPeople would make an interesting magazine story.

The *Fast Company* editors were intrigued. A few months later, in April 1999, the magazine featured a three-page article about life in the Thinkubator. The 769-word article in *Fast Company,* which included a color photograph of Haman dressed as his superhero alter ego "Solutionman," was directly responsible for landing nine clients, eight of them Fortune 500 companies.

Let's trace the web of connections from that single, evangelistic response Neil Kane posted in reply to Dan Pink's question as shown in Figure 9.2 and the 12 steps depicted in the figure.

1. Dan Pink posts a question to a Company of Friends list.

2. Neil Kane notices the post and forwards it to Haman.

3. An article about Haman is written for the magazine.

4. An employee of Adidas reads the *Fast Company* article and calls Haman for more information. Adidas becomes a client.

Figure 9.2 | Web of Connections from One Evangelist

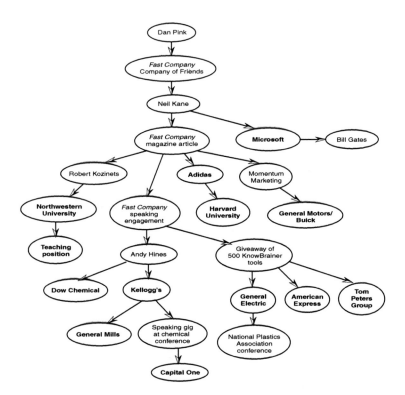

Source: SolutionPeople

5. An employee of Adidas loves the work and evangelizes Solution-People to contacts at Harvard University, several of whose MBA graduates eventually become SolutionPeople clients.

6. A representative of a company called Momentum Market-ing reads the article and decides SolutionPeople is just what its client, General Motors, needs. Several weeks later, the Buick division of GM joins the SolutionPeople client roster.

7. *Fast Company* invites Haman to speak at its 1999 RealTime conference in Naples, Florida.

8. At the conference, *Fast Company* gives away 500 Know-Brainer tools to attendees. The tool giveaway is central to landing new clients General Electric, American Express, and the Tom Peters Group.

9. At the RealTime convention, Haman meets Andy Hines, who at the time was with Kellogg's. Several weeks later, a team from Kellogg's journeys from their Battle Creek, Michigan, headquarters for a session at the Thinkubator. Their brainstorm eventually produces new cereal products.

10. Hines departs Kellogg's and joins Dow Chemical. Shortly thereafter, Dow becomes a SolutionPeople client.

11. Hines evangelizes Haman's company to his peers in the chemical industry, and eight months later Haman is speaking before the Chemical Specialties Conference in Chicago.

12. Sitting in the front row at the conference was an executive from Capital One, the financial services firm. The executive liked what he heard and shortly thereafter a Capital One team was jamming in the Thinkubator, brainstorming new products and ideas.

All told, one evangelist—Neil Kane—was indirectly responsible for at least $2 million in revenue for the small business of Solution-People.

Kevin Olsen is the founding partner of One Smooth Stone, a marketing firm for the meetings and events industry. In 1995, Olsen took the same calculated risk Haman had three years earlier by investing several thousand dollars in a trade show as a bet-the-company marketing strategy. But the trade show he'd bet on, the

Chicago Society of Association Executives, was a bust. "We couldn't catch a cold there," he says. "And we only met one person. It was Gerald. We were ready for Gerald."

It turns out that Olsen and his young company needed the systematic approach toward creativity and innovation that Haman offered. The two became fast friends. Olsen involved Haman in several of his company's projects, and as they worked together, they referred clients to one another. There was Xerox, A.T. Kearney, Navistar, Motorola. Olsen quickly grasped the idea of evangelism marketing— it turned out that he is the son of a preacher.

"An evangelist is one of the highest callings there is," he says. "I am an evangelist of what I believe in: building relationships that win. Gerald is a classic example of a relationship that will have legs for a long time."[12]

The power of the media can be exponential, and Haman has created a solid strategy to help journalists quickly accomplish what many of them seek: a good story about a colorful character. He sends the KnowBrainer tool to reporters before an interview and uses it during the interview as a live demonstration of the tool's effectiveness as well as for providing reporters a new avenue for asking questions.

The first article about SolutionPeople in 1989 created ripples of subsequent articles that continues years later. Haman met Linda Stockman-Vines, a journalist who writes about training, human resources, and creativity issues, in 1989 at the ASTD conference in Dallas. Intrigued, Stockman-Vines wrote an article about the Know-Brainer tool for *Human Resource Executive* magazine. We can trace the effects Stockman-Vines had on Haman's business and the roots of SolutionPeople at the 1989 ASTD convention by examining Figure 9.3 and a chronology of the 12 steps represented in the figure.

1. Haman rents a booth at the ASTD conference in Dallas.

2. Five hundred people purchase the KnowBrainer tool (known then as the Pocket Innovator).

Figure 9.3 | Early Roots of SolutionPeople

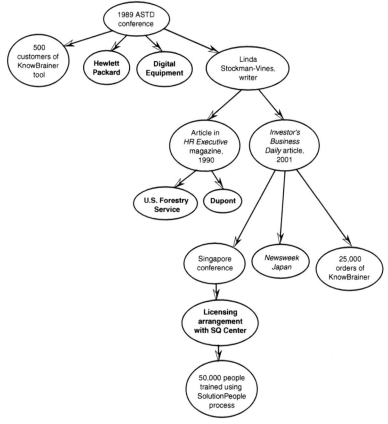

Source: SolutionPeople

3. Hewlett Packard and Digital Equipment Corporation become clients.

4. Haman meets writer Linda Stockman-Vines.

5. She writes an article about Haman for *Human Resource Executive* magazine.

6. Executives at Dupont and the U.S. Forest Service read the article and sign on as SolutionPeople clients.

7. In 2001, Stockman-Vines writes another article about Haman, this time for *Investor's Business Daily.*

8. An official with the government of Singapore reads the second article and invites Haman to help brainstorm government improvement strategies, which leads in turn to setting a Guinness World Record.

9. The Singapore conference leads to a KnowBrainer licensing arrangement (and one of Haman's key strategic objectives) with a Singaporean company.

10. The Singapore licensing arrangement trains 50,000 people in Asia using the SolutionPeople approach.

11. *Newsweek Japan* publishes an article on Haman's company; an Indonesian consulting firm that reads the article licenses the KnowBrainer tool.

12. Haman sells thousands of KnowBrainer tools because of the *Investor's Business Daily* article.

Gerald Haman is not afraid to be out there. To dress up in a costume; to stand out in the crowded business field; to introduce theater into business. That's when he becomes Solutionman, who sports a red cape, tights, and a sturdy chin not unlike Haman's boyhood hero, Superman. Solutionman was born when Lari Washburn, one of Haman's clients at Lucent, said out of the blue one day, "You're such a solution man." That was another lightbulb moment, and soon Solutionman was being photographed for *Fast Company* magazine, making appearances in schools, and canvassing trade shows. An appearance at Chicago's Francis Xavier Ward grade school in 1997 created a good deal of buzz. Solutionman teaches kids in various Chicago schools several times a year about the value of teamwork and creativity. He also has pictures made with the kids he teaches, and the pictures are developed with a Solutionman sticker on the back. One photograph caught the attention of a parent who wondered what the Solutionman business was about and called Haman for more information. The parent, a lawyer for a large Chicago-based law firm, liked the pitch and thought the American Bar Association could use Solutionman's help. Soon, the ABA was a client; later the parent's law firm itself became a client as well.

The creation of Solutionman is part of a larger network of connections in the history of Haman's company that began years earlier with Haman's membership in Chicago's Museum of Contemporary Art, as depicted in Figure 9.4 and explained in the following 11 steps.

1. Haman joins Chicago's Museum of Contemporary Art.

2. He becomes active in the museum's group of art evangelists.

3. His involvement with the group introduces him to several future clients: R.R. Donnelly, the large printing company; and two advertising agencies, J. Walter Thompson and DDB.

4. His involvement with the museum inspires him to pursue his hobby of painting.

5. His hobby results in two exhibitions.

6. At one of the exhibitions, Haman meets two future clients, Helene Curtis and Discover Card. He is also invited to participate in another art exhibition called Around the Coyote.

7. At another exhibition, he meets his future wife, Jillian.

8. At Around the Coyote, Haman meets Val Mrak, a film producer, who introduces him to Mary Borse, at that time an employee of AT&T, which later becomes a client.

Figure 9.4 | SolutionPeople Buzz Map

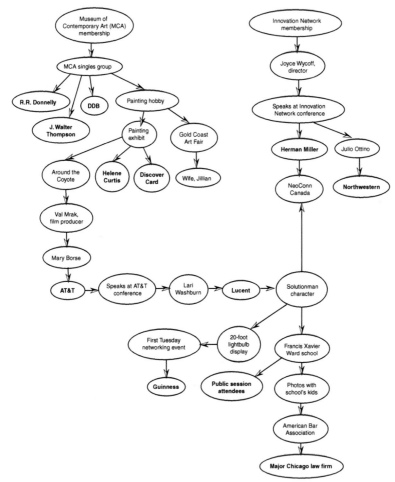

Source: SolutionPeople

9. AT&T invites him to speak at a conference, where he meets Lari Washburn of Lucent, which soon becomes a client. His work with Lari leads to the development of Solutionman.

10. At an appearance at a Chicago school, Solutionman's picture piques the interest of a parent, who eventually helps Haman

land new business with the American Bar Association and a large Chicago-based law firm.

11. Solutionman inspires the creation of a huge lightbulb display, which gets the attention of a Chicago networking group, First Tuesday, and eventually leads to landing another client, Guinness UDV, the beverage company.

After each major event, SolutionPeople posts a 100-page, picture-heavy PowerPoint document on its Web site. The photos prominently feature people and the event's accomplishments. A 20-person event held at an English castle in March 2002 generated 5,000 viewings of the online document, Haman says. A common element among our seven case-study companies is an unwavering emphasis on an enjoyable experience. A utilitarian experience is not memorable, but an enjoyable and fun experience creates buzz. A day at the Thinkubator, Haman's name for his studio where people journey to brainstorm ideas for their companies, gets people talking. I (Jackie) signed up for an Accelerated Innovation seminar held in October 2001.

Once inside the Thinkubator's front door, I'm mesmerized. A toy frog at the entrance delivers a welcome croak. The room is a colorful splash of life. Everything from the furniture—large red-lip chairs and comfy couches—to the dozens of lightbulbs-as-idea sculptures to a bathroom whose tub doubles as a tank for Solutionfish creates brainstorm sparks. It's like stepping into Pee Wee Herman's Playhouse minus the talking chair. I can't wait to talk about everything in the room being crazily out of the ordinary.

It's 8 AM, and the other workshop attendees are already jazzed; music jukes the background. We settle in on the comfy funky couches and beanbag chairs. Haman introduces himself to our group of 25. We are marketing specialists, organizational development consultants, executives of associations, and managers of various companies in and outside of Chicago. We learn this will be a bite-size chunk of what Haman's Fortune 500 clients pay up to $100,000 to experience over several days.

Haman explains that one day during his junior year at the University of North Dakota he arrived late to his philosophy class. His professor, Dr. Benjamin Ring, was not pleased and asked Haman to consider the question "What motivates people?" By the end of class, Haman had written that question over and over until he filled 25 pages of his notebook. (Interestingly, Dr. Ring had also posed the same question to a previous student, former NBA star and renowned coach Phil Jackson.) In 1981, the question of what motivates people burned inside Haman's mind, eventually driving him to launch Solution-People. The answer to the question: being creative.

Thanks to a study by a graduate student at Northwestern University, Haman learned that people are 13 percent more productive when not wearing shoes, and 20 percent of people think faster when standing. Haman invites us to remove our shoes and slip on brand-new white tube socks that he gleefully distributes. Everyone is quite amused.

It's time for work. We begin with the "Know Your Brain" game. We file into a room filled with color-coded cards—blue, red, green, yellow—each of which has a word imprinted on it. We are told to pick three cards that best describe ourselves. I select two reds (Enthusiastic, Passionate) and a green (Planner). We file back into the main room and introduce ourselves, our colors, and why we chose the colors we did. As I circulate in the room, I make connections with my fellow reds, knowing that we belong to a community of passion.

Haman keeps the motivation mojo going by announcing he will distribute tickets to those who actively participate in today's session by asking questions or volunteering. (It seems Dr. Ring has taught him well.) At the end of the day, he will conduct a drawing for prizes for people who gather the most tickets. Immediately, we're intrigued. Win prizes? This is going to be fun.

Haman tells how Einstein was once asked, "If you were given an hour to save the world, how would you spend the time?" Einstein said he would spend 55 minutes investigating the problems and 5 minutes coming up with ideas.

Haman says, "Judge intelligence by the answers given to questions. Judge creativity by the questions asked."[13] This is a segue into the "Question" game. We are each to pair up with someone and practice using the "Flash Word" technique, just as Haman does with real reporters. I pair up with John, whose firm helps companies improve shareholder value. One of us is to play the "reporter" and the other an "expert." Using the KnowBrainer tool, John plays reporter first and randomly asks questions from each of the four steps in the process. I'm stumped by several questions. The KnowBrainer surfaces issues I would have never imagined, especially in my profession.

The challenge is dialed up a notch because John takes satisfaction from playing mean reporter. I find the KnowBrainer questions such as "What do you want people to feel?" and "What do you want people to think?" interesting because they're uncommon. John throws in his own, with some derision: "Why would anyone care about what you do?" I guess that my answers don't immediately add up to shareholder value. I decide that John could have a new career on Fox News.

Now it's time to form "colorful teams of twisted thinkers." We organize into groups of four and five. Our mission is to apply Haman's Diamond Solution Process to a problem. We tackle "how to choose a Halloween costume." Our group does OK in the investigative and creative steps, but falters in the evaluative step, and we're not sure why, even though our problem seems straightforward. The metaphor of how this happens every day in companies across the world—settle on an idea and move forward—is not lost on us.

By now it's time for lunch, which is being served in the Thinkubator's disco, which is part dance floor and part carnival. Freed from our natural adult states, we play with some of the toys, such as the basketball shoot. Music, of course, is playing. We gather around three large round tables with white tablecloths and heavy silverware. The food is gourmet and so is the conversation. When I ask the eight people at my table how they heard about Haman and SolutionPeople, they reply it was from another person. Most are here to experience the Solutionman's creativity and brainstorming exercises firsthand as a toe-in-the-water reconnaissance mission to evaluate SolutionPeople for a full, three-day session, or to hire Haman as a speaker for their conference. All have paid to be here. The idea of the bite-size chunk works beautifully for the Thinkubator.

After lunch, it's time for karaoke. We divide into teams and take turns singing lead and backup for several songs that everyone knows. There's nothing quite like belting out "Takin' Care of Business" at the top of your lungs after lunch to stave off the effects of turkey sandwich tryptophan. We venture back to the Thinkubator to work through the Diamond Solution Process on our individual projects. Once finished, Haman poses a to-the-point question: How many of us brainstormed an idea that will make $5,000? $10,000? $50,000? One participant says his idea could generate $1 million. This has everyone's attention. By positioning our work in terms of returned revenue, Haman deftly illustrates the relationship between creativity and making it pay. Marketing is the same; it should have well-defined returns for each idea invested.

Then it's on to the Thinkathon. He distributes sheets filled with lightbulbs that represent ideas for a problem that's posed at the top of the sheet. Each lightbulb represents an idea of how to tackle the problem. Haman tells us about his customer at Abbott Labs, the large pharmaceutical company: The customer tapes Haman's lightbulb sheet to the door of his office, with a problem/challenge at the top. All visitors must add an idea to the sheet before entering his office. Haman distributes sheets filled with drawings of lightbulbs. Our challenge is to think of ways to introduce more creativity into our workplace. We have three minutes to brainstorm ideas. When our time is up, we pass our sheet to the person on our left and add ideas to the problem that has just been handed to us from the person on our right.

It's the end of the day and time for the prize drawing. Good thing, too; by now we're brain-dead. Prizes are think bars, lightbulb toys, squeezable brains, and Einstein paraphernalia. Haman gives everyone a hat that looks like a brain, designating us as "brainiacs." An expert marketer, Haman reminds us about the value we received during this day of creativity and that we'll receive an e-mail survey asking us to rate the session. Even though we're exhausted, many of us find it hard to leave. We're in a cool and creative space, where we had fun, led by a warm and smart leader, and we met some great people. Some linger to inquire about Haman's ability to help them with their companies. For many of the assembled participants, leaving meant going back to a job and office politics and a decided lack of creativity. Armed with the tools and knowledge of the session, they hope to change that. All of them will tell others about the workout their brains received.

Evangelism Scorecard: SolutionPeople

Customer Plus-Delta

- Every customer is given the opportunity to grade her experience.

- Quantitative and qualitative data is gathered, collated, and reviewed.

Napsterized Knowledge

- The KnowBrainer tool is a handheld encapsulation of Haman's methodology.

- By creating an interactive experience, Haman has provided the means and the tools for customers to conduct better brainstorms in their own companies.

Build the Buzz

- A unique product spreads buzz quickly.

- A positive and fun experience spreads buzz quickly, especially with the media.

Create Community

- Participating at the Thinkubator is joining a community for a day.

- Displaying talents within a community creates connections.

Bite-Size Chunks

- For those who are uncertain about investing $100,000 for a dedicated session, a company representative can first attend a daylong public session for several hundred dollars.

Create a Cause

- Haman launched his company to help people discover their creative potential.

CHAPTER TEN

O'Reilly Media:
The History Lessons of
O'Reilly's Wars

People are going to change the world and accelerate change
by spreading their knowledge.[1]

—Tim O'Reilly, founder and president of
publishing company O'Reilly Media

Sebastopol, California, was named after a fistfight. Legend has it that in 1855 an argument between two early settlers in northern California, Jeff Stevens and a man known only as Hibbs, erupted into fisticuffs. It was a lengthy match, with Hibbs taking the majority of punches thrown. Beaten and bloodied, Hibbs staggered in retreat to the general store, barricading himself inside for the rest of the day. Thwarted after several hours of waiting him out, Stevens finally went home a victor but defeated by Hibbs's retreat.[2]

The spectacle of the fight reminded amused onlookers of the Crimean War, which had been raging half a world away. Back then, the French and the Russians disagreed over who should have access to trade routes in the Middle East. Czar Nicholas of Russia wanted to protect his religious shrines along the routes at all costs. As disputes involving religion often do, the disagreement erupted into war. Britain and France teamed up to take on the Russians. Britain's Florence

Nightingale tagged along as a medical technician, eventually changing the nature of nursing.[3] The French and the British chased the Russians all the way back to the Russian naval base of Sevastopol and could have considered their mission accomplished and gone home. But they didn't. At Sevastopol (where the *v* is favored over the *b*) the Russians picked off the British and French like ducks at a hypnotic pond. Their barricade was impenetrable, and Nightingale had her hands full. Two years later, the British and French gave up and went home defeated. The primary lesson of the Crimean War: Don't be greedy.

How ironic then that 144 years later a few residents of quiet Sebastopol, California, had their own Crimean War. This time the battle was with an Internet giant to the north, Seattle-based *Amazon.com* and its founder, Jeff Bezos. Amazon was granted a patent for its "One-Click" buying process, which can significantly reduce the time required for online purchases. Amazon wanted to enforce its patent and make its biggest competitor, Barnes & Noble, stop using a similar process. Fear that Amazon would enforce its patent against other Web sites also using a one-click program filtered across the Internet. It was like Czar Nicholas seeking to protect his trade routes at all costs.

Tim O'Reilly decided to step into the fight. He is the founder and CEO of O'Reilly Media, a publishing company based in Sebastopol, California. From its beginnings as a technical writing consultancy, O'Reilly Media has blossomed into arguably the most respected technical publisher today. Its growth has fueled an expansion into medical, travel, and bioinformatics titles; conferences; and a brief foray into software. With 300 employees, O'Reilly Media is the biggest company in Birkenstock-bucolic Sebastopol—a $65 million company in 2000. Tim O'Reilly describes his calling as an idealist who rallies technology mavens around causes that improve technology and its community of enthusiasts. When *Amazon.com* was granted its One-Click patent, O'Reilly began receiving calls asking to organize a boycott of Amazon. Instead, O'Reilly sent Bezos an e-mail that read, in part:

The technologies that you have used to launch your amazing success would never have become widespread if the early Web players, from Tim Berners-Lee on, had acted as you have acted in filing and enforcing this patent. Because, of course, you are not the only one who can play the patent game. And once the Web becomes fenced in by competing patents and other attempts to make this glorious open playing field into a proprietary wasteland, the springs of further innovation will dry up. In short, I think you're pissing in the well.[4]

O'Reilly says that Bezos replied with a terse "corporate brush-off" e-mail that held Amazon's ground. Undaunted, O'Reilly created a petition to protest Amazon's patent, which he e-mailed to several influential technology leaders, encouraging them to sign and forward the petition to people in their networks. "I knew that if I sent this e-mail message to a few people, they would reflect on it, and I would get . . . critical mass all at once, where all these people are hearing the same message at the same time," O'Reilly says. "It's a refinement of the principle that if you can get that critical mass of recognition coming from multiple directions at once, you're in good shape."[5]

Two days later, O'Reilly's evangelism for the cause had resulted in collecting more than 10,000 signatures. The signatures were paired with thousands of comments, such as "Dear Mr. Bezos: I think that your efforts to maintain and enforce the One-Click patent are a mistake, which makes me question whether I want to continue working with *Amazon.com*."[6] Bezos paid attention. After a phone call with Bezos that O'Reilly describes as cordial and informative, Bezos agreed to drop his enforcement of Amazon's One-Click patent. Like Florence Nightingale 150 years earlier, Tim O'Reilly had saved Amazon from itself while evangelizing a convenient feature of Internet commerce that many take for granted today. It's this caused-based leadership in a public arena filled with posturing and wrestlerlike catcalls (where most of the participants lack muscle tone and all of them wear glasses) that has made O'Reilly Media a leader in its field. It has also been a large component of the company's marketing strategy.

Tim O'Reilly's advocacy of technology causes began in July 1996 when Microsoft had just pissed him off. Back then, Microsoft had two versions of its high-level operating system available: NT Workstation and NT Server. Whereas NT Server was the more feature-rich of the two, both could function as Web servers. At the last minute, Microsoft changed the TCP-IP code on NT Workstation so that no more than ten computers could connect to it, essentially rendering it useless as a Web server. The upshot was that Microsoft doesn't own TCP-IP code; no one does. It's maintained by a volunteer group of programmers who help set and write to industrywide computer standards. Microsoft's tactic effectively blocked Web-based software, including O'Reilly's, from being hosted on Microsoft's less expensive, yet popular, platform. Its ploy was to force owners to upgrade to the more expensive NT Server, which had no limitation on connections. For Tim O'Reilly, Microsoft's action was a gambit to take control of the Internet.

"I was outraged," he says. He channeled his outrage into a protest campaign that prominently featured him in several dozen news stories, including an appearance on CNN that he feared "went over most people's heads."

"I sent an open letter to all of our customers. I asked people to let Microsoft know this was cheesy. Microsoft got an awful lot of mail. I got an awful lot of mail from inside Microsoft saying 'Thank you for helping to do this. There's been a lot of internal debate here.'"[7] A week later, Microsoft conceded to the protest campaign and removed the technical limitation. In the end, O'Reilly said, the only difference between the two products was "about three lines of code in the registry." A month later, in August 1996, the U.S. Department of Justice received a formal complaint from an ad hoc consortium of technology companies about Microsoft's actions; history shows that O'Reilly's protest over NT Server was the opening act in an odyssey that culminated in 2001 when a federal judge declared that Microsoft was, indeed, a monopolist.

From the experience, O'Reilly realized that courting customers to be active participants in a cause that is of mutual benefit to company and customer is a central tenet of his business philosophy. "This was accurate some years later in the whole Amazon patent protest—the idea of mobilizing a customer base. There is a level where you can have customer activists, people who care about the topic. A lot of what makes it work is that we draw our authors from the same customer pool. A classic statement about a market is . . . that it is a group of customers who reference each other when making buying decisions."[8]

Indeed, his company's marketing philosophy was crystallizing around this idea. At a publishing conference where he was asked to describe next-generation products such as e-books, O'Reilly shared his epiphanous moment: "I said what's beyond the book is 'life and having an impact.' We got more and more excited about this idea that our fundamental mission wasn't to publish books. It was to capture knowledge and evangelize technologies. It was to capture the knowledge of innovators. People are going to change the world and accelerate change by spreading their knowledge."[9]

Sara Winge, O'Reilly's vice president of corporate communications, says of her boss: "Tim is real. He's coming from a belief of what's right."[10]

O'Reilly explains his interest in rallying his company around a cause another way: When he first met with distributors to sell his company's books overseas, he attended a prospective partner's executive conference; most of the talk was about money.

"I was just appalled," he says. "I said the reason you guys are always number two is because the only common language you have is money. All that your people talked about in this conference was how much money they were making or not making. There was no vision. If you follow the vision, you'll catch up on the money side."[11]

O'Reilly's advocacy on behalf of the open source community earned him Infoworld's Industry Achievement Award in 1998. Asked to explain the roots of his activism, O'Reilly talks about his life. He was born in Cork, Ireland, in 1954. His father was an Irish-born neurologist, but the only way he could obtain a research professorship was if someone died and opened a slot. So the family moved to the United States when O'Reilly was six weeks old. As a teen, O'Reilly was a painfully shy "total nerd" and "the only kid who could strike out at kickball." Puberty and drama helped change that. "I remember the first time I was on stage: My eyes would close down like the end of a Warner Brothers cartoon," he says. "I was close to fainting. I eventually trained myself to be an extrovert."[12] After high school, it was on to Harvard to study the classics. His honors thesis explored the tension between mysticism and logic in Plato's dialogues. O'Reilly notes that his wife, Christina, has been "a major influence"; her values are the company's values. "This whole idea that the company is a meeting point of some work that's to be done to meet the needs of a group of people really came from her," he says.[13] With a wave of self-discovery having curled up to the shore, O'Reilly pauses. "Business is ultimately providing value. I look for the sweet spots where idealism meets making money."[14]

Because O'Reilly trained himself to be an extrovert, to be out there and take the stage for what he believes to be right, the lens of customer evangelism automatically is stronger and more focused.

The 7,700 residents of Sebastopol live in the heart of California's rich and sprawling wine country, 90 minutes north of the gleaming glass and satin metal office parks along Highway 101 that make up what is popularly known as Silicon Valley. The 168,000

square feet spread among the three buildings that make up the head-quarters of O'Reilly Media could easily be at home among ski cha-lets in Aspen. Built in 2001, company headquarters are very new; the rich aroma of new millwork fills the hallways. There's nothing of-fice-park-like about the design and the layout, although there's plenty of room for the company to grow into. The visitor lobby showcases the O'Reilly library of titles, a programmer's dream hutch. It's filled with the colorful spines of O'Reilly's technology books and the iconog-raphy of the animal etchings that identify most of the techie titles. Those bread-and-butter manuals cover a diverse range of subjects: *Programming Perl to SQL In a Nutshell* to *P2P Networking Overview* to the best-selling *Missing Manual* series.

The company's strategy is to court the communities of technol-ogists whose livelihood depends on the technology concepts and code reviews in its books and manuals.

One courtship tactic is to publish 35 various and specialized weekly e-mail newsletters that cover topics like Linux, Java, and Perl; there are special newsletters for librarians, professors, and book retail-ers as well. Each newsletter has its own voice imparted by an editor who is free to stamp his or her personality on its content. The news-letters also avoid a pushy sales approach. Tips are popular topics in O'Reilly newsletters, too, such as "Tips for Building Web Database Applications."

The company also actively courts the extensive online commu-nities of technologists, such as the millions of people who each month visit *slashdot.org,* a news and community site that posts links to arti-cles of interest to programmers and engages in Web-based discussions about technology issues.

Jeff "Hemos" Bates, *slashdot.org's* executive editor, says that Tim O'Reilly's advocacy of technology causes is recognized by *slashdot.org's* community. "I think Tim's taking a stance on issues has definitely helped them," Bates says. "It has established [O'Reilly Media] as a company in which the management still 'gets it' and cares about the concerns of its readership. But frankly, it's the accessibility and intelligence of the people writing their books that really helps them. Those people, while having other jobs, burnish [O'Reilly Media's] name because they are smart and connected with the community."[15]

O'Reilly Media learned how to connect with communities at a deeper level because of Brian Erwin, who had spent several years at HarperCollins in San Francisco and William Morrow in New York, marketing books like Alvin Toffler's *The Third Wave* and Christina Crawford's *Mommie Dearest*. Then came a call from the Sierra Club, a 700,000-member activist organization whose mission is to "explore, enjoy, and protect the planet," and Erwin launched its national media operation. It was a cause that suited Erwin well. His idealistic parents were "always taking in foster children or Peruvian refugees—it was just the nature of how I was raised," he says. "Each of us has an obligation to help those who aren't as lucky as we are."[16]

While at the Sierra Club, Erwin trained individuals and groups to fight companies and change government policies that needlessly harm the planet's ecosystem. Being surrounded by "the largest collection of Type A, outer-motivated, intelligent people I've ever been around" was an "incredible experience," Erwin says.[17] He joined O'Reilly Media as its director of public relations in 1992, just before the company published *The Whole Internet: User's Guide and Catalog*. It was a fortuitous engagement. Erwin used the tactics he had learned at the Sierra Club to market O'Reilly's products beyond its obvious channels.

"Before [Brian], we would have just sent the book out to regular trade magazines," Tim O'Reilly says.[18] O'Reilly says that Erwin recognized the importance *The Whole Internet* could have for readers in understanding the role, capabilities, and potential of a global Internet with future implications for communications, commerce, and community. Erwin pursued coverage in such national media as *TIME* magazine and the *New York Times* and sent copies to every member of Congress. According to O'Reilly: "Brian really crystallized it for us because we were always part of a technical community. If you've ever done body surfing, you can see the waves coming. The point is, the essence of surfing is catching a wave at just the right moment and letting it carry you. A lot of customercentric marketing is catching waves. It first means watching the waves and being in touch with your market. One problem is that marketing is seen as an add-on as opposed to something that's intrinsic to the way you develop your products. While Brian got us to think about activism, we were on very fertile ground because we were already seeing ourselves as a voice of a community. We were writing the books for a class of people we knew really well because we were them."[19]

The Whole Internet was one of the first two books about a technological phenomenon that eventually spawned thousands of books, hundreds of magazines, and millions of Web sites. But the manuscript kept getting delayed, Erwin says, so in the summer of 1992 he decided to print 1,000 copies in its manuscript form to launch a grassroots campaign. He sent 500 copies to various media outlets and 500 to the moderators of news groups mentioned in the book with a personalized note attached that "would say 'We hope you enjoy this and we hope you'll speak well of it to others who are visiting your news group or mailing list.' Pretty soon we could see on the Internet that people were saying, 'Hey, we were mentioned here.' It spread exponentially."[20] Erwin's strategy of identifying and targeting key influencers worked.

"That really is where the first wave of demand came from— from those who were already using the Internet,"[21] he says. The second wave came from the efforts of sales director Jill Tomich, whose grassroots activism with the company's network of retail booksellers turned corner bookstores into hubs for disseminating Internet information. She mounted campaigns that resulted in bookstores dedicating and naming shelf space for their growing list of Internet books, thus driving what became a multi-million-dollar publishing program.

Combining Erwin's evangelistic efforts with global media and financial markets with Tomich's local grassroots campaigns converged into a perfect storm of product demand. The book was selling 25,000 copies per month, Erwin says, and eventually sold more than a million copies. The New York Public Library named it "one of the most important books of the 20th century." The book eventually changed the nature of O'Reilly Media altogether. "It lifted the whole company financially and provided a focus for its next area of emphasis, which was away from operating systems and more towards mass communication," says Erwin.[22]

For Tim O'Reilly it was a marketing approach that codified the development of future programs. The search for key influencers started the process that "we have formalized as an evangelist program," O'Reilly says.[23] The O'Reilly evangelist program was launched in September 2000, with Simone Paddock named its first director. "We saw that there was a possibility of seizing part of the marketing power in the community; we needed someone to create the community around O'Reilly,"[24] she says. The program, which is by invitation only, rewards the company's most visible evangelists with books, T-shirts, and discounts on O'Reilly conferences. An O'Reilly evangelist is thus ordained because he stood up in an online discussion area, or a chat room, or in an Amazon book review and professed love or admiration for an O'Reilly title.

Although the company cannot specifically measure the effects of its evangelist program, it does have supporting evidence. Since the launch of the program, traffic to the company's Web site has more than doubled. During the first year of the evangelist program, O'Reilly's Web sites were featured more than 70 times on *slashdot.org;* 20 of those notices were a direct result of an ordained O'Reilly evangelist. Considering that a single mention on *slashdot.org* can drive tens of thousands of visitors to a featured Web site, the evangelist program is spreading the word.

In 2002, the company launched the "O'Reilly Irregulars" program. For most publishers, understanding how much inventory exists in bookstores is a considerable, if not impossible, challenge. The "Irregulars" program relies on customers to report each month on how many books are sitting on the shelves of bookstores in medium and large cities. Within 72 hours of the program's announcement, the company had almost 300 volunteers. "We think one of the things that makes us stand out from our competitors is that we're better at listening to and talking with our customers," O'Reilly says. "We know that the people who read our books and Web sites and attend our conferences are also the people who are pushing the envelope of technology itself. They are the ones who lead, shape, and contribute to technical communities. Our mission is to pour fuel on the fire they're building."[25]

O'Reilly Napsterizes significant levels of specific knowledge outside a standard $39 technical book. The company maintains a network of multiple Web sites filled with tools, knowledge, and information for programmers and information technology executives on a variety of techie topics. For example, there's *perl.com* for people interested in the Perl programming language, which is used extensively for e-commerce and moving data back and forth between a Web browser and a database. There's *xml.com,* a resource site to learn, and stay current with, extensible markup language, often called the next generation language to power the Internet. Each year, O'Reilly Media hosts several conferences, including the O'Reilly Open Source convention, where 2,000 people powwow over the direction and future of software that's written by a global community of developers. The company's other conferences, on emerging technology and bioinformatics, attract 400 to 500 attendees. Gathering these customer communities together is a key part of O'Reilly's marketing strategy that provides O'Reilly's customers a chance to meet other customers under the O'Reilly banner, plus it creates a forum for the company to understand which issues are important to its customers. Tim O'Reilly and the O'Reilly Media employees use the conferences to gather feedback and input on existing products and services.

"Ideas grow in value as you spread them often," O'Reilly says. "People worry that they'll be totally ripped off . . . [but] you can tell people virtually anything and know you're safe. If somebody out-executes you, it's a good incentive to you."[26]

Much has been made of the future of e-books and other computer-housed books whose promoters have said could mean big changes in paper-based publishing. While the major e-book programs to date have failed to gain traction, O'Reilly partnered with six other technical publishers to launch the "Safari" online book program in 2001. Designed as a subscription service that puts the contents of its popular titles online, an entire manuscript is searchable; online tools allow the titles to be annotated and bookmarked. Like Napster, the company's digitized intellectual property has a streamlined and faster channel of distribution. Is O'Reilly concerned about his company's intellectual property moving through cyberspace without traditional control structures in place?

"It certainly has to happen where we give away ideas and some-body comes along and does better with them, but I go, hey, it's part of the game. I once gave a talk at some publishing conference and the Borders buyer said, 'Well, you just gave all your competitors their program for the year.' I just go out and say, 'Here's what I think is interesting' as opposed to 'I'm going to play my cards close to the vest.' Somebody once said to me, 'The reason I like O'Reilly is because you don't have too many MBAs who have figured out that you're not doing it right.'"[27]

The company gathers feedback through three primary channels: e-mail, trade shows, and its customer call center. O'Reilly says that gathering feedback at trade shows is "a virtuous circle because you're visible. You have people come to you. If you're not visible, you have to actually go out and solicit information."[28] In 1986, before the World Wide Web was born, O'Reilly recognized the potential of e-mail as a customer feedback touchpoint. He included his e-mail address at the time—DECVAX!adelie!ora!tim—in books and encouraged readers to send him feedback. "You have got to have a product that makes people feel attached," he says. "The virtuous cycle keeps going if people get what they expect. Build expectations. You have this great community market. People feel betrayed when you let them down. That's part of the customer dialogue. The most successful open source projects are those that have . . . effectively made an efficient market and status, where people get acknowledged a lot—they get this positive feedback loop. We've done a lot of the same thing by getting our customers involved, giving us ideas, being involved in contributing to our books, writing the books. When the products are available, we already have this group of people who are already invested."[29]

O'Reilly defines the need for customer involvement as a core component of the overall human experience. "If you give people some sense that they contribute, then it's like a gift," he says. "They want that. There's some sense in which customercentric marketing is letting people be part of something bigger. That whole impulse to say, 'I'm part of something big, I'm part of something successful, I'm part of some movement,' is a very natural human impulse. By getting our customers involved, giving us ideas, contributing to our books, writing the books, we have this set of people who are already invested when the products are available."[30]

One of O'Reilly's heroes is Harold, the last of the Saxon kings of England in 1066. Harold had promised William of Normandy—perhaps under duress—that he had no desire for the crown. Yet sure enough, Harold had been ordained king of England. An upset William was out for revenge and launched an attack in the southern part of Harold's kingdom. "Basically, all of Harold's advisors were saying—when William was raping and pillaging . . . in the south of England—take your time. Regroup. Get your troops together," O'Reilly explains. "Harold clucked, 'That's not the deal. These are my people.'"[31]

So Harold sped his exhausted troops south and met William in Yorkshire for the famous Battle of Hastings. Harold and his troops fought gallantly, knowing their lives and possibly the future of England was at stake. History asserts that had Harold let his southern kingdom die so that he and his troops could regroup, perhaps he and his troops would have defeated William. O'Reilly says the story of Harold the Saxon king, motivates his approach to customers. "I feel like we owe our customers something," O'Reilly says. "It's not just what we're selling them. If you want your customers to be loyal to you, you have to be loyal to them."[32]

Evangelism Scorecard: O'Reilly Media

Customer Plus-Delta

- Tim O'Reilly encourages readers to e-mail him directly with ideas and suggestions at *letters.oreilly.com.*

- The company uses its conferences as a forum for understanding macro and micro trends related to its industry as well as its customers.

Napsterized Knowledge

- The company's Web site *www.oreilly.com* is a vast pool of information and knowledge that extends well beyond its published books.

- Safari Tech Books online brought together many technical book publishers to put book contents online as a subscription service *safari.oreilly.com.*

Build the Buzz

- The company features non-techie animal etchings on its covers.

- Tim O'Reilly uses the Web to extensively communicate issues to the community.

- A strong focus on relationships with bookstores resulted in the creation of O'Reilly bookstore "shrines."

Create Community

- The company invites evangelists into an exclusive evangelism community.

- The annual O'Reilly conferences bring customers together under the company's umbrella.

- O'Reilly's various e-mail newsletters keep customers communities in the loop on issues large and small.

Bite-Size Chunks

- Its expansive Web sites feature excerpts from books as well as updated information.

Create a Cause

- Tim O'Reilly campaigns on behalf of open-standards software and encourages the development of the open source movement.

The Dallas Mavericks: The New Mavericks of Marketing

Treat every customer like a god. Gods will introduce you to other gods.[1]

—Dallas Mavericks owner **Mark Cuban**

Mark Cuban is a rebel with a cause. He's out to make life better for long-suffering Dallas Mavericks fans. He wants to overthrow the elitism of the NBA, introduce new levels of marketing sophistication to the sport, and bring fans closer to a game that has declined in popularity since 1997.

Since purchasing the Mavericks in 2000 for $285 million ($200 million for the team and $85 million for part ownership of the arena), Cuban helped revive a dormant franchise into a winning team—both on the court and in the back office. Take-it-or-leave-it fans have morphed into a raucous group that encouraged the team to reach the second round of the NBA playoffs in 2000, the first year of Cuban's ownership. The last time the team had made the playoffs was in 1990. The Mavs made the playoffs five straight years after Cuban bought the team, even making it to the NBA finals in 2006 for the first time in franchise history. They lost to the Miami Heat in six games, but that season was indisputably the greatest in the team's 26-year history.

Cuban is one of the most visible and approachable professional sports team owners in the past 20 years. He attends every Mavericks game and sits courtside, cheering his team on and hollering at the referees. During home games in Dallas's American Airlines Center, the scoreboard flashes his e-mail address: *mark.cuban@dallasmavs.com.* After games, he's often seen in the arena's two-level bar, hobnobbing with hundreds of fans and downing dozens of Diet Cokes. You won't see him wearing a tie; it's often a jersey or a T-shirt. For a billionaire, he doesn't dress like the stereotype.

He's not afraid to speak out, which sometimes gets him into trouble. Cuban has a knack for converting missteps into positive publicity. As "The Dairy Queen Guy," he was the billionaire who stuck his size 11 foot in his mouth; his continuous complaints against the NBA's consistency in officiating culminated in an off-hand remark that he wouldn't hire the NBA's chief referee "to manage a Dairy Queen." As we recounted earlier, what could have been a PR disaster turned into a PR bonanza of Cuban "managing" a Dallas-area Dairy Queen for a day.[2]

Cuban's media-fueled ubiquity has its critics. Sports writers have the most enmity for Cuban's invasion of what he calls "the NBA country club." *Dallas Morning News* columnist Kevin B. Blackistone summarizes the media's love/hate relationship this way: "He has played those of us in the media just as adroitly as he has played the NBA commish. He has had us turn him into arguably the most famous sports team owner in the country, right up there with George Steinbrenner and Jerry Jones, but for all the wrong reasons. Steinbrenner and Jones made their celebrity primarily by winning. Cuban is making his primarily by whining."[3]

The team's success on the court since Cuban took over in 2000 has certainly been a big part of renewed fanaticism and improved fortunes. In the 2000–2001 season, the team finished 53–29 and made it to the conference semifinals, with 20 of its 41 regular-season home games sold out. Between December 15, 2001, and the end of the 2005–2006 season, the team had 198 consecutive regular season home sellouts (233 if you include playoff games). Despite the Mavs' success on the court, it would be difficult to argue that Cuban's kinetic ownership and visibility have hurt the bottom line. Season ticket sales in 2006 increased 112 percent since the 2000–2001 season, and merchandise sales increased 300 percent. Sponsorship revenue increased 176 percent during the same period.

Forbes reports that the Mavs' valuation as a franchise increased 26 percent the year Cuban took over. A year after that, the valuation rose another 35 percent. The business magazine ranked the franchise the 15th most valuable of the 29 in the NBA in 2002; by 2006, the team was ranked 5th overall. In four years, the team's valuation went went from $211 million to $403 million, and annual revenues increased from $68 million to $124 million. As an NBC-TV commentator said during a televised Mavericks playoff game in May 2001, "Thanks to the Mavericks and Mark Cuban, Dallas has become a basketball town." That's a feat, considering the Dallas Cowboys have commanded the majority of sports fans' attention in Dallas for decades.

A believer in customer evangelism shepherds more believers into the flock. This is true whether one has the capability and fortitude to own a professional sports team or not; the lessons here seem ideally applicable to medium-sized companies with high profile talent and visibility, especially in the entertainment industry, which is where Cuban says he competes. The evidence shows that the entertainment value Cuban brings to the court is packing the pews with throngs of believers.

Mark Cuban is a bags-to-riches story. Originally from Pittsburgh, Pennsylvania, and the grandson of Russian immigrants, Cuban demonstrated an entrepreneurial aptitude at an early age. When he was 12, Cuban asked his father for new basketball shoes, but the elder Cuban challenged him to earn them. His father's poker buddy suggested selling garbage bags door-to-door in the South Hills neighborhood of Squirrel Hill. Cuban didn't hesitate. "Who can say no to a kid selling garbage bags?" Cuban asks, recounting his first paying job. "No one said no. They were cheap-ass garbage bags for $6 a box, and I would go back once every couple of weeks and refill 'em. I had my little garbage bag route."

Other jobs included selling magazine subscriptions and greeting cards door-to-door and a stint as a box boy at a drugstore. "You name it, I've done it."[4] He dropped out of Pittsburgh's Mount Lebanon High School, which, oddly enough, didn't prevent him from enrolling at, and later graduating from, Indiana University with a business degree. At Indiana, his entrepreneurial ambition continued; he gave disco lessons and started a chain letter that paid for his junior year's tuition. He pooled his college financial aid with the money of friends and opened Motley's Pub in Bloomington, Indiana.

Cuban's penchant for challenging conventions began at IU. During his freshman year, he enrolled in the business school's graduate courses because he thought they looked interesting. Today's more sophisticated computer-based college enrollment systems would prevent such an occurrence, but in the late 1970s Cuban took graduate-level courses in entrepreneurship, accounting, finance, and statistics. Wayne Winston taught the statistics class, and Cuban later recruited him to be his secret statistician to evaluate NBA referees' performances.

"By the time I was through with my sophomore year, I had a year and a half of my MBA done," Cuban says. Then the dean of the business school found out. "I'll never forget; he starts poking his finger in my chest going, 'I don't know what the hell you did or how the hell you got away with it, but you are going back to undergrad. This is bullshit; you can't make a mockery of the school,'" Cuban remembers the dean telling him.[5] Broke and unsure of his future after graduation, Cuban took up residence with six other guys in a three-bedroom Dallas apartment. He launched computer consultancy Micro-Solutions without any backing. Cuban's sales charm helped him land customers even though he didn't know much about computers or programming. "Oh, you want that done in dBase? No problem," he says, explaining how he would close the sale and then cram all night learning how to program dBase.

Seven years later, MicroSolutions was grossing $30 million a year. He sold the company to CompuServe for $5 million and then played the stock market for about a year. One day in 1995, friend Todd Wagner wondered aloud, "Wouldn't it be great to listen to Indiana University basketball games over the Internet here in Dallas?"[6] Thus, AudioNet—later renamed *broadcast.com*—was born, sowing the seeds of Cuban's eventual membership in the billionaire boys club; he and Wagner sold the company to Yahoo for a reported $5.7 billion. Cuban's take: a reported $2 billion. Cuban was one of the few Internet pioneers who sold out before the tech bubble burst. If luck and timing were the names of an intersection, Cuban would own all of the surrounding property.

Now that he had pole-vaulted onto the lists of the richest Americans, Cuban considered his options. He set out to buy Napster, but Bertelsmann beat him out before he could finalize an offer. There was his passion for basketball—he was, after all, at Indiana during basketball coach Bobby Knight's heyday. Cuban met with then Mavericks owner Ross Perot Jr., and through a series of meetings, Cuban, the expert salesman, convinced Perot to sell the Mavericks. They announced the deal on January 4, 2000. Cuban says the purchase wasn't a business investment so much as a "decision of passion."

That jibes with what Rick Alm observers. He is a reporter at the *Dallas Morning News* and has covered the high-dollar world of sports ownership since 1994. Alm says Cuban's formula for successful ownership has two ingredients: "passion and impatience."

"He's very focused on who his audience is," Alm says. "As you walk around town, you get a casual sense of his personal involvement. That's translated very well into the fans' opinion of him. And it helps that he has dramatically improved the team."[7]

After a game in Dallas one balmy night in January 2002 in which the Mavs had just lost to the Los Angeles Clippers, we corraled a group of fans. Some of them were what the Mavericks call "Painted People," those who paint their faces and bodies in Mavs' regalia. We asked for their opinion of Cuban's work. (See Figure 11.1.)

Figure 11.1 | Dallas Mavericks' Painted People Fans

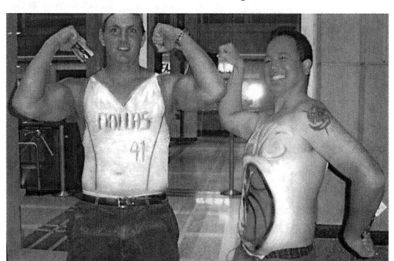

Chris Bontrager (left) and Todd Walley have been fans of the Mavericks through good times and bad. With Mark Cuban as the team's owner, being a fan represents the good years, they say.

"He's the man!" says Todd Walley, emphatically. Walley has painted his entire face in Mavericks blue. A pretty good rendering of the team's basketball-and-pony logo covers his bare belly. "He's the only team owner who comes down to games in blue jeans and T-shirts. He's not stuck up. He's one of us, you know?"[8]

Chris Bontrager painted his bare chest to resemble a Mavericks uniform. He has been a fan "ever since he can remember." Fandom was tough during the 1990s, Bontrager says. It's different now. "Cuban has brought the buzz back to Dallas for basketball," he says. "It's a complete 180. Everybody's excited about the team again."[9]

Besides his penchant for body paint, which he calls a fun outlet to "go out and get loose," Bontrager says he persistently lines up friends to attend games and generate enthusiasm for the team. "Oh yeah, I try to persuade them all the time," he says.

George Killebrew is the Mavericks' vice president of corporate sponsorship and a back-office veteran since 1991. He says fans compete for Cuban's attention with homemade signs as much as they compete for the attention of players. "We used to have a rule in the old arena that you couldn't bring a sign in because it would obstruct someone's view," Killebrew says. "Is that what you really want if you're marketing entertainment and sports?"[10]

Cuban's personal involvement means many things. First among them: Do not behave like a typical owner, perched in a skybox with the rest of the well-heeled crowd. Although he usually sits near his team courtside during home games, Cuban joins fans in the $8 seats high above the court five to ten times a season. He chats with anyone who approaches him, devoid of handlers, obliging every request for an autograph or picture. This provides Cuban the opportunity to discover what his customers like and love, loathe and hate. He'll shoot a series of quick questions to the fans for quick temperature gauges: "How's the parking situation? How's the food? Who's your favorite player?" When he took ownership of the team, the Mavs held a strong command over last place in its division. During the 1992–93 season, when Don Carter owned the team, the Mavs' record was 11–71, two games shy of tying a terrible NBA record. On his first day as the new owner, Cuban called season ticket holders on the phone and asked them to hang in there, promising that improvements would be coming soon.

To create what he calls "a fresh look for a fresh start," Cuban updated the team's logo and uniforms, which hadn't been updated in the team's 21-year history. The change process normally takes a full year, but Cuban and his back office team changed the logo, all marketing materials, and uniforms between seasons. "That's a good example of his impatience and desire to get things done," Alm says

"Not any of the other owners would have done it like that."[11] Nor would many owners have introduced the new uniforms using a fashion show motif, complete with a runway. Cuban did, using two of the players as models. Nor do most team owners personally market the products of their other customers—the team sponsors. Cuban does. He advocates and appears in ads for Body Solutions, a weight-loss product, and Planet Tan, a tanning company.

"He'll always go the extra mile for his sponsors," Alm says.[12]

During the 2000–2001 playoffs, the team offered free admission to fans who painted their faces in the team's colors. The next season, the Mavs launched its Painted People section as a full-scale, season-long program supported by a corporate sponsor. Painted People cheer 30 rows up from the floor in a section where seats typically cost $51 each.

Then there's *The Mark Cuban Show*. The team's local television partner pitched the idea and "upped their offer for the Mavs TV package if I did it,"[13] Cuban says. Once a week, Cuban hosts a 30-minute . . . how shall we describe this . . . variety show. He promotes the players, coaches, ticket packages, himself, and the Mavericks dancers. Tapings are held at a local watering hole and are open to the public. At a January 2002 taping, Cuban works the room before, during, and after the show. He has a smile, a wave, a finger point for everyone who catches his attention. Coach Don Nelson is that night's guest. On the air, Cuban asks him to recall their first meeting.

"I thought you were probably going to let me go," Nelson says.

"Were you having fun at that point?" Cuban asks.

Nelson laughs. "No, I wasn't."

"Are you having fun now?" Cuban asks.

Nelson smiles. "Hell yes," he answers.

Cuban wants fans to know his e-mail address—in case you missed it earlier, it's *mark.cuban@dallasmavs.com*. Every day, about 1,000 e-mails fill Cuban's computer screen, and he contends he answers every one unless it asks for money or a job. A nightmare to some, but Cuban loves it. His e-mail inbox is a well of ideas. For example, one day in 2001 Cuban received an e-mail from a fan who had attended a game but had trouble seeing the 24-second shot clock perched above the basketball net's glass backboard. The clock was designed for players to see, not necessarily fans. How about a three-sided shot clock so everyone in the arena could see, the fan suggested. Several weeks and $24,000 later, brand-new, three-sided shot clocks were perched above the backboards of each basket. Most of the NBA has since adopted the idea. Fans e-mailed Cuban saying they had trouble getting to the arena's box office. A twisty maze of roads off Stemmons Expressway southwest of downtown Dallas leading to the arena box office can be confusing even for locals. The team responded by opening a satellite ticket office downtown with easy parking.

"Rule number one of any business is listen to your customers," Cuban says.[14] Other ideas from fans that have become Cuban action items: fixing broken seats, improving the signage in the arena's parking lot, ensuring that hot dogs are hotter and beer is colder, and stopping fans from trudging up and down the aisles while the ball is in play.

More evidence that basketball is more entertainment than sporting event is the way Cuban coaches his sales team to sell an experience and entertainment, not a win-loss record. He argues that people who attend a sporting event "don't remember how many passes were thrown." "You might remember something that was artistic—a big dunk, a great run, a homerun, or a throw—but you remember how you felt," Cuban says. "The things you remember are what you felt inside, and that's what we sell. The thing I spend the most time on is trying to work on the experience in the arena. That's what I focus on the most because that's where I control my own destiny. It's all about the game experience because it's like throwing a party every night. You can't run out of beer at a party."[15]

Having owned a bar during his college days, Cuban would know. During home games, Cuban often dashes from his seat to the scorekeeper's desk. He says it's to keep the arena video and audio technicians who mix in music, sound effects, video snippets, and prerecorded cheers alert to each event associated with the game. In fact, he usually recommends specific music and video selections. "You might see me mad at the refs, but you'll see me madder if it's a critical part of the game and they're not playing 'Let's go Mavs' or 'Defense,'" Cuban says. "You'll see me stand up and run over to those people and say, 'Get it going!'"[16] By dedicating resources and energy to the overall experience, not just the players on the court, Cuban and his substantive back-office team say they can do their jobs better.

"It matters not who our opponent is or what our record is, whether it's against the [Los Angeles] Clippers on a Tuesday night or the [Los Angeles] Lakers on a Saturday night," says George Prokos, the team's director of new revenue. "Bottom line: There's no excuse why we don't fill the building every night."[17]

The customer experience at American Airlines Center often extends beyond basketball. The team has booked live music performances to immediately follow some games. In 2001, a postgame performance by country music singer Pat Green helped fill 6,000 unsold seats. The concert strategy worked well during the 2000–2001 season, when six concerts brought in $50,000 to $80,000 each. Even though the team broke even on the effort, the bigger strategy was to bring in more people to experience the spectacle of a modern-day basketball/entertainment extravaganza.

The team creates bite-size chunks of its season ticket program by allowing fans to purchase five-game or ten-game ticket packets. During the 2000–2001 season, the team sold 7,000 "mini-plans," as they are called. Thirty percent of the plan purchasers upgraded to a half-season program and 25 percent upgraded to a full season.

At the onset of his ownership, Cuban gave his team a goal of making it to the playoffs within two years. It worked. They made it in one. He also added 30 additional salespeople to an existing staff of five. There were 4,800 season ticket holders when Cuban bought the team; two years later, that number quadrupled to over 16,000. Like any successful leader, he executed his strategy every day using incentives and enthusiasm, not fear and intimidation. Cuban capitalized on the team's underdog status. He played up his role as a "fan-based owner," the outsider who's just a fan at heart. It seems the team's players connect with their boss, too. At 7 feet and 6 inches, center Shawn Bradley is the team's tallest player and also one of its veterans. He's been a Maverick since 1997, three years before Cuban bought the team. What's different now?

"The team mood is one of confidence," Bradley told us, just before the team was readying for the playoffs for the second time in two years. "The Perots were great owners and wonderful people, and I think everyone on the team liked them, but they approached the team from a real business aspect. Cuban does that too, but he also adds an element of confidence and player support that is unique to any team that I have been on."[18]

Teammate Greg Buckner was also with the team prior to Cuban's arrival. Of Cuban he says, "On the basketball side of things, he has made a complete turnaround."[19]

Cuban defines his cause as excellence and fun. "I want to have fun, I want to be the best, and I want to make a lot of money doing it. It's that simple."[20] It's a bit deeper than that. Continuing in his tradition of challenging everyone, Cuban says his role is not to please NBA commissioner David Stern, who has fined him ten times for $1,455,000 and suspended him from three games for speaking out. (It's more than that when one factors in that Cuban matches each fine with a donation to charity.) Cuban's larger cause is making the NBA exciting and entertaining again. Attendance at NBA games has been in decline since 1997, when an average of 17,135 fans attended each game. During the 2000–2001 season, that average was 16,778. That same season, Dallas jumped from 11th to 8th in attendance among all NBA teams, with an average attendance at 16,589. By 2006, the team was ranked third in attendence with average attendance of 20,121.

Cuban's whistle crisis with NBA officiating is a smaller part of his cause. Deeper still, Cuban considers corporate culture a root problem of what troubles the league. "You have to set the culture because that's how people make decisions," he says. "If you don't know what your cause is, if you don't know what your culture is and what you're rewarded for and what's respected and what's expected, then you'll make mistakes when you let people make judgments. Then you get all kinds of autocratic environments that don't succeed."[21]

Matt Fitzgerald is responsible for all of the Mavs' marketing and communications. A former senior marketing manager at Coca-Cola Company, Fitzgerald first met Cuban in 1999 playing basketball at a Dallas gym. Over the course of their weekly basketball diaries, Fitzgerald asked Cuban if he should accept a promotion Coke was offering. Cuban told him to instead consider working with the Mavericks. During a meeting in which Fitzgerald presented a formal "Restaging the Mavericks" plan, Cuban offered this sports industry outsider the job of chief marketing Maverick.

"Instead of selecting a marketing person from the NBA or the sports industry, Mark consciously made a decision to hire someone from outside the industry," Fitzgerald says. "He believed the NBA marketing community was too inbred so [Cuban] was looking for a marketing person with a fresh perspective and ideas."[22] Like his billionaire boss, Fitzgerald focuses on customer communications to build and maintain goodwill. "We answer every e-mail that comes in. The whole organization answers e-mail."[23] In an e-mail to Cuban in January 2002, a fan suggested a promotion to capitalize on all-star forward Dirk Nowitzki's recent and impromptu head-shaving. During warm-ups before a game, Nowitzki had dashed into the locker room to have his head completely shorn of its ample blond locks. Cuban forwarded the fan's idea to Fitzgerald, who was happy to report they were already building a plan.

A few weeks later, the team launched a promotion for fans to shave their heads for charity—in this case, breast cancer research and treatment. Held on the night the Mavs played the Los Angeles Clippers, 75 fans lined up to get their heads shaved in exchange for a free ticket. The idea landed ProCuts as a corporate sponsor to join the team's existing roster of 100 other sponsors. So fastidious is the team's awareness about the marketing allure of its players that a team employee scooped up all of Nowitzki's shorn hair from the locker room floor and auctioned it for charity, Fitzgerald says.

This move-fast mentality is based on what Fitzgerald calls "real-time feedback." "We don't subscribe to a lot of the traditional types of research—focus groups—because we see this arena as a giant focus group every night," he says. "We're not afraid to try things. Quite frankly, a lot of things we do don't work but it's OK because we just move on. It's all about doing a lot of little things."[24]

After the Mavs had lost two key games against the Utah Jazz in the 2001 playoffs, Cuban told his back-office team that he would purchase up to 2,000 tickets for fans to attend the next game in Salt Lake City. The catch: fans had to find their own way to Utah and paint their faces in Mavs' colors. The next morning, Fitzgerald and his team flooded Ticketmaster's phone lines, scooping up 680 tickets. The team announced the promotion on its Web site, and in 45 minutes 1,500 fans were ready to make the trip. In Salt Lake City, Fitzgerald gathered the fans at a hotel across from the arena, threw a party, and guided them to surround the team's bus as it arrived, cheering the players on into the arena. Did it work? The Mavs came back from being 17 points down in the third quarter to win the game and advance to the second round of the playoffs.

"It's just rapid-fire," Fitzgerald says of their marketing approach. "For a sports team, it's really buzz marketing that works best. It's [Cuban's] style, and it works really well for us."[25] The way it works: Every day Cuban filters his e-mail for ideas. He forwards the ideas he likes or the complaints that should be heard to the appropriate department head, usually with a brief action comment.

"You know how a lot of organizations behave where everybody is filtering up to the top?" Fitzgerald asks. "Here, it's the inverse. Everything comes through him, and he filters it out to the organization. The momentum swings so quickly. You have to be very flexible and ready to just jump on things when they become available." Fitzgerald says the flexibility comes from not having an ironclad marketing budget and plan.

"We're a completely idea-driven organization," he says. "If there's an idea to have a fun party to get people going, we do it. That's not to say that Mark funds every idea.

"In the world I came from, there was a lot of vacillation back and forth—should we do it, shouldn't we do it. With Mark, it's just an e-mail away. He could say, 'That's stupid, that sucks, no way.' Or he could say, 'I love it. Go ahead and do it.' We just move. We move. We move. We move."[26]

Cuban keeps things moving by demanding weekly e-mail reports from his back-office team. "And the bad news has to go first," Cuban says. "For a salesperson, if they're losing a customer, boom! I want to see the customer we lost because that's the trigger item. I'm always looking for the trigger item, what's going on that I need to understand."[27] To keep his marketing and sales efforts responsive, Cuban says that "you'll never see me do branding, ever. I'm a big believer that you go for the call to action and that if you're providing value and you let people know about the value, then your marketing takes care of itself."

That also means no meetings. "I am Mr. Anti-Meeting," he says. "I hate meetings. Everybody postures. You create a report, and you're just going to read it to me. Just send it to me and I can read it sitting on the toilet in the morning."[28] Cuban's 30 salespeople also rely heavily on fans for referrals and help. "You'd better be asking for referrals in everything you do," Cuban says. "The underpinning is that you treat every customer like a god. Gods will introduce you to other gods. "Being a good company is like being a good lover: First you ask your partner what they want, then you give it to them. Then you ask them if they liked it. If they say yes, you give it to them again! That's what customer service is all about: being good to people. If someone enjoys the experience, it makes them look good to tell somebody else. If you focus on one, it leads to the other."[29]

Asked if he has transferred the idea of marketing on "Internet time"—a reference to the instant communications approach prevalent on the World Wide Web—to the Mavericks, Cuban replies: "It's about customers' time. We all live in a world where everything happens in real time. You have to move at the speed that your competitors are moving. There's always a new movie, there's always a new restaurant, there's always a new opportunity. That's my competition. If I don't move, then I'm going to lose."[30]

Competition for entertainment dollars—where Cuban says he competes—is fierce. To succeed, he says he must continually focus on increasing the average lifetime value of a Mavs season ticket holder. In 2002, that figure was $300,000, according to Cuban. "The [Chicago] Cubs, you've got to wait in line to get your season tickets," he says. "That's the goal . . . then I don't have to spend lots of money on salespeople and all kinds of support efforts—I've just got to keep [customers] happy. It's a lot easier to keep 'em happy than to go out and get new ones to replace 'em."[31]

The Mavericks' marketing is not just for fans and corporate sponsors; the team also markets itself to players on other teams. After all, with the realities of midseason trades and free agency, today's most reviled opponent could be tomorrow's star forward. In the visitors' locker room at American Airlines Center, the settings are roomy and luxurious. For a while, visiting players were given their own towels and robes, free for the taking. But the NBA put a stop to that during the 2001–02 season.

The Mavericks' locker room resembles an expensive health club: beautiful wood, carpet, pool table, leather couches. Game films are viewed on large, high-definition televisions. A weight room rivals those found at large downtown gyms. Each player's locker comes equipped with a flat-screen TV, a CD/DVD player, stereo system, and a Sony Playstation. Surprised that the team was viewing game films by threading actual film into a projector, Cuban commissioned a system to digitize the films and make them viewable on PCs. This allows coaches and players to study opposing teams' games on their laptops while at home, traveling, in the whirlpool, wherever.

The word is out.

"Just recently I heard a few of the other NBA players talking about how this is the place that other players want to come and play for," Shawn Bradley says. "Some players want to be a Dallas Maverick because of the environment and the situation that Cuban has created here."[32]

The Mavs' Greg Buckner says Cuban's work has "set the standard for other owners in the NBA. Other teams are now trying to match what he has done and what he continues to do so they can compete in the free agent market."[33]

The team's investment in technology extends to tickets, too. A common problem for many sports teams is sellouts that aren't sellouts. Scores of empty seats often belie announced attendance figures. At each home game, every used ticket is scanned for a unique bar code that tells the back-office team who attended and who didn't. The next day the team calls a ticket owner to say, "Hey, we missed you last night," Prokos says. "Is there something we can do to enhance the experience to help ensure you use those tickets?"[34] Although declining to divulge specific numbers in what they call their "drop count," Prokos says the effort has a "marked difference" for improving attendance.

Finally, there is the January 2002 Dairy Queen incident. Both organizations skillfully turned a verbal slam into a marketing slam dunk. Now when an opposing player or coach is ejected from a game, they are "DQ'd," much to the delight of new sponsor Dairy Queen.

"Part of the point I was trying to make with the NBA is that you have to understand your customers and learn to get better as a business," Cuban says.[35] Did it help the NBA? Perhaps. Did it help the Mavericks and Dairy Queen sell more stuff? Hell, yeah.

Evangelism Scorecard: Dallas Mavericks

Customer Plus-Delta

- Cuban encourages fans to send him e-mail. Many contain suggestions for improvement.

- The Mavericks' Web site has a bulletin board filled with thousands of comments.

Napsterize Your Knowledge

- "The more you try to hide information, obviously the more things you have to hide," Cuban says.

Build the Buzz

- Cuban publicly voices NBA issues to generate discussion.

- The team's marketing group capitalizes on fast-moving opportunities—the Dairy Queen incident and Dirk Nowitzki's shaving his head, for examples.

Create Community

- By encouraging and rewarding fans for decorating themselves in the team's colors and logo, the team engenders a deeper bond with fans.

- Dallas Mavericks Foundation Community service (Hoops for Hearts program with the American Hospital Association).

Bite-Size Chunks

- The team offers five-game and ten-game ticket packets as an introduction to full-season ticket ownership.

Create a Cause

- Cuban publicly lobbies for changes in the NBA's strategies and tactics.

- The Mavericks back-office team creates an entertaining fan experience, knowing that that they are selling fun, not wins and losses.

Build-A-Bear Workshop: A Bear Market for Retailing

Every single one of our customers is engaged in the process of making Build-A-Bear Workshop more famous by telling someone about their experience.[1]

—**Maxine Clark,** founder and chief executive bear of Build-A-Bear Workshop

The early years of the 21st century were difficult for some long-standing players in the retail industry. Montgomery Ward, retail visionary, initiator of the mail-order catalog, and inventor of the catchphrase "satisfaction guaranteed or your money back," filed for bankruptcy and closed for good. Born in 1872, it died in 2000. Kmart, pioneer of discount retailing that began life as Kresge's, filed for bankruptcy in 2002 and announced it was closing 284 of its 2,114 stores. More than 22,000 employees were fired. Born in 1899, Kmart was struggling to survive but eventually recovered when a hedge-fund operator purchased the company in 2003 and merged it with another faltering operator, Sears. It took a few years but both Sears and Kmart eventually refound their financial footing as a combined entity.

Analysts said Wards died and Kmart and Sears nearly died because of consistently poor customer service, miscalculated growth strategies, and too much retail supply with not enough demand. Exceptionally high levels of retail space available in 2002 added to the problems.[2] U.S. Bancorp Piper Jaffray found that from 1998 through the end of 2000, retailers added nearly one trillion square feet of new store space to the American retail landscape. That caused retail profit margins, already at a thin 4 percent in 1996, to fall to 0.01 percent by the end of 2000. Satisfaction among retail customers was among its lowest point ever then, too. The American Customer Satisfaction Index, which is compiled by the University of Michigan, found the retail industry had never surpassed a baseline satisfaction score set in 1994. That spelled doom for some but an ideal opportunity for others.

Like Maxine Clark. She soared through the retail industry downturn hitched to a rocket she'd created called Build-A-Bear Workshop, a St. Louis–based retailer of stuffed animals. In 1997, when she first launched the store, total first-year sales were $377,600. Four years later, Build-A-Bear had grown to 75 stores and over $100 million in sales. During that time, a Build-A-Bear store rang up about $700 per square foot; the national mall average was $350.[3]

Clark was no lightweight newcomer to the industry. As president and chief merchandiser of Payless Shoe Source from 1992 through 1996, she gave that retailer legs: she increased annual revenues from $1.5 billion in 1992 to $2.3 billion by 1996 was overseeing a network of 4,500 stores with 24,000 employees. Payless became the number one seller of kids' shoes in the world. During her presidency, one out of six pairs of shoes bought in the United States were from Payless.[4] As a decades-long executive of The May Department Stores Company (the parent company of Payless as well as Foley's and Lord & Taylor, among others), Clark understood retail as well as anyone. But something was missing. Theater. Emotion. Connection.

"With Build-A-Bear Workshop, I am trying to go back to the way businesses used to be when they really focused on the customer from a personal perspective," Clark says.[5] Childhood shopping memories resonate strongly with Clark, who turned 58 in 2006. When Clark was a child, her mother, Anne, would take Maxine and sister

Sharon on hour-long shopping trips in downtown Miami. In the early to mid-1950s, shopping was an event. That added to its memorable nature.

"We used to window-shop for entertainment," Clark says. "We would get dressed up—even wear hats and gloves sometimes. We would have lunch downtown, and it was special. The stores always had something going on."[6]

One store that forever captured Clark's imagination was Burdines. William Burdine opened his Miami general store in 1898; 104 years and 52 stores later, it's called "the store of Florida" because it has never expanded beyond its home state. In the 1950s, a rooftop circus was a big draw for Burdines. An attached gift store called the Little Shop was for kids to buy presents for their siblings. "Everything was really low—you could reach it—it was all done kind of like Santa's toyland," Clark says. "I have never forgotten that in my entire life, and it's the standard by which I measure everything that I do."[7]

Her turn-back-the-clock approach is propelling her forward. Clark won the 2001 Retail Innovator of the Year award from the Center for Retailing Studies at Texas A&M University. She was presented with the 1999 award for Emerging Entrepreneur of the Year from Ernst & Young. The International Council of Shopping Centers gave Clark's company the Hot Retailer Award for 2004. Her forward motion is helping shape the now publicly held Build-A-Bear Workshop into a global concern; its first store outside the United States opened in Great Britain in 2002, with stores in Japan, Denmark, Australia, South Korea, and France opening shortly thereafter.

After graduating from the University of Georgia with a degree in journalism, Clark opted for the executive training program at the May Company instead of cub reporting at a newspaper. Starting out at Hecht's department stores, Clark rose through the ranks as an expert merchandiser. One of her more memorable assignments was to create a gift shop for kids. She called it "The Land of Ahhs," just like the Little Shop Clark had remembered as a young girl at Burdines.

"It was really well received, and I had a lot of fun doing it, but most of the time there's just not enough room in a department store to create that type of environment," Clark says. It took 25 years as a professional retailer but it was around 1995 that Clark got "bored with shopping." Financially secure from her success, Clark quit the corporate world without a clear plan. Although Payless went public a year later and with it would have come the chance to build additional wealth, Clark says she has no regrets. Besides, the entrepreneurial bug had bitten, and she wanted plenty of time and room to figure out her next move. She investigated buying a Krispy Kreme franchise in St. Louis, but that effort didn't pan out. Her research took her to a toy factory in China in 1996. Although she doesn't remember its name "because it was in Chinese," the factory offered tours to schools, so Clark says she tagged along on one. "When I went on the tour, I saw a special look in the children's eyes that said

Figure 12.1 | **Build-A-Bear Workshop**

Children participate in the manufacturing of their own toys at Build-A-Bear Workshop.

this idea had more potential," she says.[9] The words of her late mentor, the May Company's chairman Stanley Goodman, rang in her ear, too: "When customers have fun, they spend more money."[8]

With fun in mind, the idea that took hold was to reinvent the concept of toy manufacturing inside a mall-based store. With $750,000 of her savings, Clark opened the first Build-A-Bear Workshop in the St. Louis Galleria in October 1997. Venture capitalists have supplied an additional $12 million to develop a store that's unlike most others, much less one that caters primarily to children and 'tweens, that group of kids between 9 and 12. A Build-A-Bear Workshop store is about 3,000 square feet, the size of the typical Gap location. There are no chattering robots, toy guns, or Barbies—just dozens upon dozens of unstuffed animals ($10–$25) lining the brightly colored walls with a few hundred outfits ($3–$15) resembling teeny baby clothes, ready for outfitting. Once a customer has decided on a favorite "skin," as the store associates call them, it's time to begin the 30-minute life-giving process to the customer's new creation.

Working with a store associate whose official title is master bear builder, customers fill the bears' skins using a boisterous stuffing machine that resembles a large movie theater popcorn maker. Customers select a soft and tiny red heart, personalize it with a wish and a kiss, and stuff it in with the stuffing. Customers can select a prerecorded voice or record their own voice on a computer chip that's encased in the toy. (Customers who create a toy on the company's Web site can record their own voice over the telephone.) A unique bar code inside each toy identifies its owner in case child and toy are separated. People who find a misplaced teddy bear are encouraged to send it to Build-A-Bear Workshop, which routes it to the registered owner. Since the company began this lost-and-found program, more than 400 lost toys have been returned to their owners each year. Lost bears have been found on highways, at stadiums, in hotels, and, of course, elsewhere in the same malls in which the bears were created. Customers give their furry new friends a good brushing and a "bath" in a bathtublike area. Instead of water, streams of noisy air gush out of several spigots.

Bear birth is not an anonymous experience in the retail woods; customers are directed to a bank of computers to create a personalized birth certificate signed by Clark. The company captures each customer's name, gender, birthday, and street and e-mail address; about 90 percent of all customers register. This step in the store experience is smartly placed away from cash registers, where customers are usually in exit mode. A "birth certificate" commemorating the purchase is printed, and all of the data is sent to Build-A-Bear Workshop's central database, which remembers to send customers yearly birthday reminders, surveys, and newsletters. After five years of business, Build-A-Bear Workshop had registered 4 million customers and sold a total of 10 million toys, Clark reports. From the data it collects, the company knows how often its best customers purchase toys and how many they purchase. With their information stored away now in the company's computers, customers proceed to the final stopping point: toy clothes. Part of the Build-A-Bear Workshop experience is the attention paid to product details, especially accessories; sneakers, for example, have real treads; the "bear binoculars" actually magnify distant objects; and pockets and purses are sewn to hold additional accessories. Those details add additional authenticity, emphasizing the feeling that the child's toy is real, an extension of themselves. Clark's strategy of involving customers in the creation of their purchases is more likely to create a vivid memory of their experience and cause them to tell friends and family about it.

"Every single one of our customers is engaged in the process of making Build-A-Bear Workshop more famous by telling someone about the experience," Clark says, adding that most new customers heard about the store from a friend or family member. "The bullseye of our business is 11-year-old girls," Clark says. "Along with 11-year-old girls come 8-year-old brothers and their mothers and 13-year-old sisters. They are our evangelists because they are bringing a lot of people with them."[10]

Customer evangelists bring new customers into Build-A-Bear Workshop stores because of the many details that add up to a memorable store experience, Clark says. It's her strategic advantage and one that too many retailers ignore. Seemingly small, inconsequential details often derail memorable experiences. First, there's the always concerning problem of "nasty bathrooms." She's a bathroom inspector and says stores disrespect customers by not maintaining them. Most fitting rooms are cramped and poorly maintained, often filled with pins and detritus. Many customers, especially women with children, avoid these messy, unsafe rooms. They would rather buy clothes, take them home to try on, and bring them back for exchanges and refunds rather than use a dressing room, Clark notes.

"If a company looked at how many people brought stuff home and brought it back . . . [they'd find] it's way more expensive to handle those transactions than [ensuring that customers] feel comfortable going into a fitting room and trying it on because the fitting room has appropriate mirrors and space," she contends.[11] Another problem is too many markdowns. Retailers have become addicted to sales, which teach customers to visit stores only when markdowns occur, creating a downward cycle of devalued products and equally devalued surroundings.

"I don't know of any department store in my area that doesn't have a sale going on every single week," Clark says, scoffing at the practice many retailers use to meet revenue targets.[12]

Because Build-A-Bear Workshop avoids markdowns, it relies on memorable experiences to create loyal customers, who visit an average of five times a year. The compensation of store managers is tied to customer satisfaction ratings. Each week, managers are notified of customer satisfaction scores, which are posted for all employees to see. Stores must meet minimum satisfaction goals to qualify for bonuses.

"These results are as important as our weekly sales," Clark says.[13]

The experience is part of the sale, fueling word of mouth. By focusing on memorable experiences as its customer evangelism strategy rather than low prices or markdowns, Build-A-Bear Workshop enhances its long-term value, an idea advocated by the National Quality

Research Center at the University of Michigan Business School. "Customer satisfaction based on low price is often fragile and highly dependent on the company's cost structure and price concessions from suppliers," according to Claes Fornell, the center's director.[14]

When asked what the big, nuts-and-bolts retailers can learn from her fast-growing success with Build-A-Bear Workshop, Clark says, "I don't care whether you make screws or sell screws, or you sell clothing . . . there's nothing a store can't do to improve its business. [Stores] can use more entertainment techniques, which are sitting right there in front of them. They just don't use them."

Because Build-A-Bear Workshop's primary audience is e-mail savvy, the company relies heavily on electronic communications. So Clark's e-mail inbox fills up with 4,000 notes a month, most of them from customers.

A wire-bound volume of 175 customer e-mail printouts received that the company provided us tells several stories. Admittedly, it's an unscientific sampling of letters, but it did provide a small glimpse of feedback. For instance, many of the letter-writers reported they had driven hours from their home just to visit a Build-A-Bear Workshop store. Their purpose in writing was to ask for a store closer to their home—some suggest specific locations. Customers often go into minute detail about their Build-A-Bear Workshop evangelism efforts, often including names of friends and family as well as descriptions of what they've said. And it appears most customers approve of store employees—at least 75 percent of the e-mails name a specific employee who made a customer's experience memorable.

Clark says that every e-mail writer receives a personal response from her or one of the company's executive team. Responding to customer e-mail is not a chore; she recommends that every executive team in the world does the same. "I would absolutely recommend it

100 percent," Clark says. "I've had people tell me they think it's low-level, that they have a person who gets paid to do that. This is my monster. I go through life telling people this because I know I have not been listened to. I think companies have such bad habits from having secretaries read letters and handle customer problems."[15]

The company eschews administrative assistants, so Clark's management team is responsible for all of its own communications. That was a bit of a culture shock for Teresa Kroll, the company's "chief marketing bear," who left the May Company to join Build-A-Bear Workshop in 2001. "Obviously, you're thinking we can certainly afford secretaries," Kroll says, laughing. "But with the electronic exposure that we have today, we can get so many things done so much more quickly [by ourselves]."[16]

Several dozen kids keep Clark updated on their school activities, the health of their bears, and their life as children with daily or weekly e-mail updates. For Clark, this is like having her own personal research lab. "They are what I call Build-A-Bear Workshop fanatics," she says. "They are very much into Build-A-Bear. They are very much into the fact that they can write to me, and I respond back to them because I care. That's my interest. Their voice is important."[17]

Those voices have created 99 percent of the company's new products, according to Clark. One customer suggestion was to add a black Labrador as a product. The company did, and in its first six months, it sold 100,000 units. The company had already been offering shoes to go with each animal. Why not add socks? a customer suggested; shortly thereafter, the company did. Another customer suggested party rooms for birthdays and get-togethers, which the company began to offer in selected stores in 2002. The company bolsters its feedback program with weekly surveys sent to customers, asking them to grade their store experience. It seems like a simple premise to ask a lot of customers every week or month to grade your performance. Why don't more retailers do that?

"I think everyone thinks they know who their customer is," Clark says. "They've been doing it the same way for such a long time.

I was part of a very successful department store company for nearly 28 years of my retail life, and we didn't know half of what I know about my customers at Build-A-Bear Workshop.

"Those things drive me to think differently about my customer."[18]

Clark calls herself a quintessential shopper. She says it's not uncommon to find her trolling the aisles of dozens of stores after work and on the weekends, buying and researching merchandising trends. A lot of buying. "My husband will tell you that I have a basement full of clothes with hang tags on them."[19] As a result, she fills out six to seven customer surveys a year, always including her name and phone number, and then . . . nothing.

"No one has ever, ever called me on the phone and said, 'Thank you for taking the time to fill out our survey, and we hear what you are saying; we'd like to find out more details about it,'" Clark says, imagining what a store executive should be saying. "That little difference can make a huge amount of difference to a store's entertainment value, and not entertainment because somebody put a piano player in the shoe department."[20]

When she was a young girl, Clark herself sat on the advisory board of a department store. Her turn-back-the-clock approach led her to launch Build-A-Bear Workshop's Cub Advisory Board, a group of 20 boys and girls 8 through 17 years old who review and suggest new products. It meets with Clark and her team three or four times a year to ensure that her stores are meeting the needs of her young and influential customers. "Their candor has driven a number of product decisions and ideas," Clark says. "They are fearless and honest. They are also far more experienced shoppers [than previous generations] and selective about how they will spend their money.

"If they approve of something, we are pretty certain to have a winner."[21]

Clark says she retired from corporate life because it became "more about meetings and markdowns" and less about customers and creativity. She decided that any new venture "would have to play to my personal interests of inclusion rather than exclusion." To her, that means a heart-based community.

"Having a heart is more than a company strategy," Clark says. "It's a way of doing business. It extends to how people are treated in every aspect of the business. It is what excellent companies know is the core to success: treating vendors like partners, treating customers like guests, treating employees like friends and family. These characteristics and values are harder to find in today's fast-paced, hard-driving business world. We're not inventing anything new; we're just trying to bring [these values] back."[22]

What permeates many businesses flush with customer evangelists: employee evangelists. The tone inside company headquarters in St. Louis is meant to reflect the values that Clark espouses. One could say it's downright dot-com. Dogs and kids are welcome amid the colorful hallways and desks. There's flexible scheduling, telecommuting, and 15 "honey days" of vacation a year. All bathrooms are equipped with diaper-changing stations. There's a playroom for kids. Titles are decidedly unstuffy. Clark is CEB: chief executive bear. (The bear puns are endemic throughout the company.) Most business cards include the word *bear* in the title. Each employee spends three weeks in St. Louis at Bear University. Classes impart "The Way of the Bear," a distillation of the company's culture, its values, and its expectations for customer service. The company's chief marketing bear says there's a perfectly good reason to devote three weeks of training for every employee.

"It's about building relationships," Chief Marketing Bear Kroll says. "It goes between the relationships of our business partners, our guests, and our associates. In building those relationships, people walk away with smiles, feel good, feel rewarded, and feel all of the things you and I want to feel every day."[23]

Clark says store managers have usually worked at other successful children's retail companies, themed entertainment parks, or restaurants. The experience of their master bear builders is more varied, "but a love of kids and an outgoing personality are musts!" In 2001, a magazine named Build-A-Bear Workshop the number one "Best Place to Work."[24]

Connecting with causes is another big part of the company's strategy. Its list of charitable causes is extensive and a reflection of Clark's concerns. There's the company's partnership with the World Wildlife Fund, whose mission is to protect wildlife and wildlands. Build-A-Bear Workshop created a Bengal tiger and a giant panda whose sales benefit the World Wildlife Fund. After three years, the company has sold 150,000 animals that have benefited the WWF. There's also the company's partnership with the Humane Society. One dollar is donated to the society for each black Labrador toy sold. A popular program with shoppers, the company sold 100,000 black Lab toys in the first six months of the program.

In 2001, during breast cancer awareness month, the company partnered with the Susan G. Komen Breast Cancer Foundation and the Siteman Cancer Center to unveil a Hopeful Wishes bear. Sales of the bear benefit breast cancer research, treatment, and support. In May 2001, the company launched a "Stuffed with Hugs" day. It encourages children to participate in social causes by inviting them into the company's stores to create a teddy bear to be donated to the Teddy Bear Foundation, a nonprofit organization that helps children in crisis. Kroll says 15,000 teddy bears created by children went to kids who live in shelters as a result of neglect or abuse.

The company created *teachme.buildabear.com* in partnership with Scholastic, Inc. Multimedia flash cards quiz kids on math and geography using all of the Build-A-Bear Workshop iconography, type usage, and color palettes. A separate section helps educators with lesson plans on "friendship and cultural awareness."

"I think the cause-related positioning we have taken shows that this company cares so much about its guests, its business partners, and social issues; and it's something that other companies should assess," Kroll says. "Where do you get the best benefit: Is it on price or on building a relationship? Build-A-Bear Workshop is all about building relationships."[25]

During a drive one night in February 2002 on the way to her home in St. Louis, Clark was deconstructing what was wrong with present-day retailing. She took precise aim at a national department store that had announced it no longer accepts returns 30 days after purchase. As a result, "I don't shop there anymore," she says. "That changed my attitude about the store. They are saying, 'We don't value your business; you are not important to us' . . . and I've spent thousands of dollars a year there." So Clark created the opposite of a typical return policy: No time limits. Full refunds. Responsive. If customers need to use the phone, no problem. "And you can be sure the bathrooms are clean, too," Clark says.[26]

Part of the company's strategy is to keep a relatively small inventory of product items, usually near 3,500. A limited inventory keeps costs down and product fresh. How does the company handle inventory that isn't selling? "We stop buying it!" Clark says emphatically. "We have very accurate testing procedures, and this rarely happens—so far."[27] If a retailer is not driven by low prices or markdowns, it must then be driven by originality and newness, Clark contends. That's what drives customers.

Part of Build-A-Bear Workshop's marketing strategy is "event craziness." There are special St. Patrick's Day and Valentine's Day bears; a "spring furry fashion show" with spring clothes; a teddy bear centennial carnival. (Teddy Roosevelt's birthday is a company holiday. The teddy bear is named after the former U.S. president, who is said to have spared the life of a bear cub during a hunting trip in 1902.) Throughout 2002, the company commemorated the 100-year anniversary of the teddy bear's creation. It's a department store for creatures of the woods.

Birthdays are a big part of the company's event marketing strategy. Because Build-A-Bear Workshop knows the birthdays of its customers (and the "birthday" of every animal created), it sends reminder notices to the parents of children 90 days in advance, "telling them it's time to plan a party," Clark says, adding that this type of tactic is turning the company into something of a direct marketer.

"We know the birthday of the people who have bought a gift and the persons to whom they are sending the gift," she says. "But mostly, people make things for themselves."[28]

The company advertises in specialty magazines, but its influence is understated, Kroll says. "Wal-Mart and Target and all those other guys have their Sunday supplements, and they spend beaucoup dollars on them," Kroll adds. "It's predictable and everyone expects it. With us, it's just not that way."[29]

The company's weekly customer surveys ask customers how they first heard about the store. According to Clark, nearly half of the customers answer it was from a customer evangelist. Adding to evidence that retail is still about "location, location, location," 40 percent of customers say they stumbled across it in a mall. The remaining 10 percent heard about the store through the media or advertising. For Kroll, whose marketing budget includes public relations, the company's Web site, and advertising, word of mouth is her most effective tool, one that largely takes care of itself. "This has been the most overwhelming and luxury situation that I have found myself in," she says, laughing. "They leave our stores in a euphoric stage, and they go home and they get online."[30]

After the events of September 11, 2001, Build-A-Bear Workshop responded by sending thousands of teddy bears to children who had lost a parent or relative in the attacks. It was Kroll's second day. She had just moved to St. Louis from New York City.

"All we did was sit in the cafeteria with the TV on, trying to think of what we could do to help," Kroll says. "The next day, we had thousands upon thousands of stuffed animals going to children with families who had suspected, or in fact knew, that they had lost a loved one. We were getting calls from the Northeast on a minute-by-minute basis asking us to please send something to comfort these children. We would just do whatever it took. There were no parameters."[32] The company encouraged kids to visit its stores and help create the emergency bears. About 11,000 in total were sent.

To respond to frequent customer questions about the proper care techniques for their toys, the company launched an annual "Bear Care Training" program in 1998. Promoted only to existing customers, the program is a popular annual checkup for the Build-A-Bear Workshop toys (including those purchased somewhere else) to fix loose and broken stitching or fluff up the stuffing.

"People start calling us in January asking when it is," Clark says. "It's a big weekend."

By providing free mending services, the store also makes it easy for customers to update their bear's wardrobe or buy additional animals. "It always exceeds our expectations [of] what people purchase" during the program, Clark says.[33]

Build-A-Bear Workshop has taken the idea of mass customization and made it a responsive, adaptable marketing strategy across a their global enterprise. For instance, customers said they wanted to dress their bears in the apparel of their alma maters. Now, each store features accessories of its nearby colleges and universities. Each store's home city is well represented by products as well.

It's as if Maxine Clark is a kid again, shopping with her mother at Burdines in downtown Miami and enjoying the rooftop circus.

Evangelism Scorecard: Build-A-Bear Workshop

Customer Plus-Delta

- The company continually solicits customer feedback, aligning it with compensation so that employees are inherently reminded of what determines their immediate future.

- Ninety-nine percent of the company's ideas for new products have come from customers. Customers are the primary source of innovation.

- The company loves e-mail and encourages customers to send ideas, suggestions, and complaints—about 4,000 e-mails arrive each month.

Napsterized Knowledge

- The company was founded on the idea that manufacturing is fun and should be part of the customer process.

- The company's Bear University employee training program is three weeks long.

- All customer feedback is shared throughout the company.

Build the Buzz

- A unique and personalized bear creation process creates buzz and word of mouth.

- A Cub Condo replaces the traditional shopping bag that customers carry around the mall.

- An extensive Web site is filled with dozens of opportunities to tell a friend.

Create Community

- Extensive relationships exist with the World Wildlife Fund, the American Humane Society, and nonprofits that support breast cancer research and treatment.

- The company makes direct appeals to collector communities with limited edition products.

Bite-Size Chunks

- Stores host parties and events for kids, some of whom are introduced to the store for the first time.

- The company offers its products through select third parties and channels, such as FTD.

- An expansive Web site, *Buildabear.com*, tries to re-create an in-store experience.

Create a Cause

- Clark launched the company with the objective of changing the American retail experience.

- The company's extensive involvement with charitable organizations tells customers it stands for a number of causes; the efforts also produce extensive favorable publicity.

CHAPTER THIRTEEN

Southwest Airlines: A Cause, Not Just an Airline

Why the hell should I spend money on focus groups?
I read every letter customers write.[1]

—**Colleen Barrett**, president and COO of Southwest Airlines

In the early part of 2001, Southwest Airlines received about 3,900 customer letters every month. Some writers complained about delayed flights, lost baggage, and other systemic ills associated with air travel. But the company estimated that about three-fourths of all the correspondents were thanking the company for good service, commending a flight attendant, or requesting that Southwest establish service in a new city.

Then terrorists hijacked four passenger jets on September 11, 2001, crashing two of them into the World Trade Center in New York, one into the Pentagon in Washington, D.C., and another in a Pennsylvania field. More than 3,000 people were killed. Even though none of Southwest's planes were involved in the attacks and none of its employees were lost in the debris of destroyed buildings and lives, the company was significantly affected nonetheless. Among the hundreds of new challenges the United States and the world suddenly faced, one was key to Dallas-based Southwest: Would the American aviation industry recover? Air travel is the engine of hundreds, perhaps thousands, of local economies. A crippled airline industry poses huge risks for the economies of the United States and other countries. After the attacks, American airspace was completely shut down for 48 hours. It took more than a week for airlines to gather their bearings after resuming flights. Worse yet, palpable fear gripped the United States, especially for air travelers. Airline passenger counts dropped dramatically.

Not long after September 11, letters to Southwest's headquarters started changing. Customers wrote letters filled with emotion, expressing sorrow for what had happened. They worried that Southwest's famous cash reserves—over $1 billion—were being quickly depleted by flying nearly empty planes. Remarkably, many of the letters included money. There were checks for $5, $10, even $500. Many returned travel vouchers or gift certificates.

"After the initial shock of the attack subsided, I began to worry about the smiling people that work for Southwest," one writer wrote in a letter among stacks the company provided for us to review. "Having said that, I want to return this $100 in SWA gift certificates that one of your customer service agents sent me after I informed him of my first and only bad experience with Southwest Airlines. I wish I could send you more than $100, but this is all I have."[2]

The company's employees were the biggest givers. They requested a fund be set up for those who wanted to pledge portions of their salary to protect their fellow employees. Total contributions were $1.3 million for what employees called the LUV fund. The goodwill Southwest had cultivated outside and inside the company since its launch in 1971 was paying off. "We have customers who have rallied to the cause of Southwest Airlines," said then-CEO Jim Parker.[3]

The spirit of Southwest is an embodiment of the freewheeling personality of the company's co-founder and chairman, Herb Kelleher, a rabble-rouser and maverick. He rides a Harley to work, chain-smokes furiously, and professes an undying love for Wild Turkey whiskey. He's a cutup who, it could be safely argued, is a free spirit.

Trained as a lawyer, Kelleher once challenged another company's CEO to arm wrestle their dispute over using the "just plane smart" catchphrase. The resulting spectacle—completely over the top with cheering spectators, television cameras, and plenty of Wild Turkey shots downed by Kelleher—was a public relations bonanza. It was a defining Kelleher moment, not only of his ability to generate publicity but also to settle disputes without involving the legal system.

Kelleher's love of specatacle extends to the company's embracing of Halloween. He has publicly donned outfits portraying himself as a wrestler, Elvis, and a band major. The company's early uniforms for flight attendants featured hot pants. Now, it's only the mannequins in company headquarters who wear the company's early Barbarella-like outfits; the company's flight attendants these days have settled into khaki pants or shorts—not as risqué as before but still unconventional compared to most other airlines.

More than 30 years after its launch, Dallas-based Southwest Airlines was a responsive army of 31,000 passionate employees. It continued to rank number one or two on *Fortune* magazine's list of the best American employers. It does $7.5 billion per year in business and has outlasted competitors big and small to build a $13 billion company valuation that's bigger than competitors United, American, and Continental combined. It has been profitable every quarter and every year since 1971. Although revenues dropped significantly in the financial quarter after the September 11, 2001, attacks, it still earned a profit of $151 million. American, Delta, United, and others furloughed 115,000 workers and lost a combined $4 billion. Southwest kept all of its employees after September 11 and paid the wages lost to its skycaps, who largely work for tips.

"We have a duty to protect the jobs of our people," Parker says of the company's decision to not join other carriers with massive layoffs.

After a remarkable 35-year run as an airline industry pioneer, Kelleher relinquished his presidency and CEO titles in June 2001, making Parker CEO and then chief people officer Colleen Barrett president. (Parker later retired and CFO Gary Kelly took over as CEO in July 2004.)

"When we were deciding how to divide up Herb's responsibilities, we decided that Colleen would take all of the smoking, and I would handle all of the drinking," Parker said in his deadpan Texas drawl.[4] Barrett started her career as Kelleher's secretary and rose through the ranks in part by sending birthday cards to employees, personally responding to customer letters, and being a tireless company champion. She is credited for shaping and maintaining the company's culture. Her analysis for the company's success: "Southwest is a cause, not a career."[5]

Part of the company's success can be attributed to its desire to keep a level of simplicity inherent throughout the complex maze that is running an airline. It only flies Boeing 737s, simplifying operations by standardizing the planes. It flies direct routes only and avoids the common hub-and-spoke passenger system, thereby making the company less susceptible to delays. It does not pay millions of dollars to be part of other airlines' computer reservation systems. The evidence for the clarity of this strategy abounds. While other airlines have struggled with huge losses, strike threats, and growing concern over customer dissatisfaction throughout their lifespans, Southwest remained profitable and hovering near the top of government-issued performance metrics. Since its maiden flight in 1971, Southwest has had only one work strike.

The company has grown almost completely organically. It has avoided owning car rental agencies and reservation systems, strategies favored by competitors like UAL Corporation, parent of United Airlines, and AMR, parent of American Airlines. The flight attendants of Southwest Airlines are well known for their sense of fun, which generates tremendous buzz; an Internet search, in fact, for "Southwest flight attendants" and "humor" yields almost 2,400 Web pages. Customers obviously love capturing the humor of Southwest and sharing it. The flight attendants have been quoted as saying:

- "Here at Southwest, we flight attendants get up real early and go to the airport so we can sign up for a flight with the most handsome pilots. When you are departing the aircraft, look in the cockpit and you'll see that today we slept late."

- "There may be 50 ways to leave your lover, but there are only 4 ways out of this airplane."

- "We will be serving meat loaf today, which you can use as a flotation device."

- "The captain will be turning down the lights as we prepare for takeoff. This isn't necessary for any technical purpose. It's just been a long day and our flight attendants don't look as lovely as they did this morning."[6]

Southwest has also freed itself from serving meals on its flights, thereby avoiding the costs associated with something that customers hate anyway.

In the fiercely competitive airline industry, it's easy to go from pioneer to chump. Some pioneers were respected for their smarts but disliked for their abrasive personalities, such as American Airlines' longtime leader Robert Crandall. Many pioneer airlines have disappeared altogether: TWA, Eastern, and Braniff are several of the better known ones to have checked out. Southwest launched its business in 1967, only to fight a four-year legal battle to get its first plane off the ground. By consistently focusing on low costs and high customer satisfaction, Southwest has led all other competitors in metrics the FAA uses to measure airline performance: flight delays, mishandled baggage, oversales, and consumer complaints.

"I was talking at the Yale Graduate School of Business some years ago," Kelleher once told an interviewer. "In the Q&A session, one of the students stood up and said, 'It seems to me you're talking more about a religion than a business.' And I said, 'If you feel that way about your business, I think that's good. That's a plus.'"[7]

~

What Southwest's customers experience begins behind the scenes. A Southwest "all-hands" meeting provides some evidence of a company that is close-knit, gregarious, and huggy. On a chilly night in March 2002, about 700 Southwest employees from a dozen different cities gathered in a Chicago high school near Midway Airport—directly under the flight path of departing Southwest jets—to hear then-CEO Jim Parker and President Colleen Barrett provide a "state of the company" update. Before the event began, everyone happily hugged one another and even strangers. Thousands of hugs were distributed and almost as many kisses—most on the cheek, others on the lips—were given and received like candy at a parade. Barrett, with her two-foot-long gray ponytail, gray knit pants, gray Southwest Airlines T-shirt, and bright red sneakers, is a prodigious hugger; on this night, employees lined up for her hugs.

Parker is all Texan: he's tall and big. In his jeans, denim shirt, and unmistakable Texas accent delivered in measured deadpan, Parker seems to be an all-business cattle rancher. But he's a lawyer, trained at the University of Texas, and had been Southwest's general counsel since 1986. When the meeting began and Parker was introduced, the crowd leaped to its feet for a minute-long ovation. After September 11, the company and the industry had endured challenges unprecedented since the dawn of commercial aviation; the audience was obviously grateful to Parker for Southwest's avoiding layoffs and remaining profitable.

He and Barrett had a secondary challenge to overcome on this night and in the years ahead: being the company's leaders after Kelleher's retirement. Parker endeared himself by telling a long and funny lawyer joke (as many lawyer jokes often do, this one culminated in the simultaneous destruction of hundreds of lawyers at once, making clear that Parker doesn't take himself too seriously).

His "state of the company" report was to the point. The company had, to date, weathered the most significant crisis in its history. With detectable emotion, he discussed the company's "duty to employees to protect jobs" and reported no one was laid off after the September attacks. When he announced that 11 percent of the company's profits had been added to the employee profit-sharing plan, the crowd erupted into cheers.

Nonetheless, Parker said, passenger load levels were still down. The company would be hard-pressed to deliver a profitable first quarter. (The company later announced an 82 percent drop in year-over-year income but managed to post a profit.) The company's situation remains serious, he said, and cost-cutting was still a top priority.

Barrett was introduced next, also to an extended standing ovation. Onstage, Barrett is a laconic cutup, part Southern sass, part Roseanne. Like her longtime mentor and boss, Herb Kelleher, Barrett says what's on her mind, the antithesis of a stereotypical Fortune 500 executive. She even enjoys whining a bit, which appears to be part of her charm. Barrett is often credited with being the glue in the company's culture. She first started work at the company as Kelleher's secretary and eventually became president. Barrett's approach is to read every customer letter and often respond to them herself. At a question-and-answer session with employees, someone asked the duo about the monetary contributions that customers made after September 11.

"I wanted to give it all back, but Jim wanted to keep it," Barrett quipped.[8] Company spokesperson Linda Rutherford said the company didn't keep an exact tally, but the total was "hundreds and hundreds" of dollars.[9]

Kevin Krone, vice president for interactive marketing at Southwest, explains the company's employee evangelism this way: "I think a lot of companies miss that you have to take care of your employees. They're not an expense item on an income statement; you can't look at it that way. They are one of your biggest assets. They can literally make or break you. Taking care of them is as important as taking care of your paying customers."[10]

Prospective employees are asked how humor helped them out of a difficult situation. Pilot candidates are sometimes asked to don Southwest shorts; the ones who see the request as fun can make it to the next round of interviews. Those who see it as beneath them end up working somewhere else. The culture inside Southwest Airlines is devoted to freedom, which the company has transferred to its marketing: the freedom to be an individual (highly encouraged) and to have a sense of humor (encouraged more).

"In our hearts, we know that we have the best employees in the world," Parker says. "The Golden Rule is pretty important here."[11]

Company headquarters features thousands upon thousands of pictures of employees on the walls of its two-story headquarters. Southwest President Colleen Barrett despises empty walls, so nearly every square foot of company walls features framed pictures of employees in action at work, pictures of their kids and families, pictures in their high school cheerleading uniforms. Like a proud mama, the company even frames its employees' artwork and hangs it on the wall.

Colleen Barrett chairs a committee of employees from every area of the company. Known as the Culture Committee, its purpose is to build on the company's effervescent personality throughout the employee ranks. The results allow Southwest to retain a familial atmosphere amidst rapid growth.

"People who emphasize too strongly the fact that they're professionals usually are not very good at what they do," Kelleher says. "What really adds up to professionalism is being very good at what you do in a very modest way."[12]

Kelleher is well known for flying on Southwest's planes to talk with customers and employees. One frequent flyer in Texas has sat next to Kelleher three times in ten years. Each time, Kelleher asked him and others nearby how well Southwest was doing in a number of areas, looking for trends, spotting inconsistencies. This strategy comes from a customer-focused belief. "We tell our people, 'Don't worry about profit. Think about customer service.' Profit is a by-product of customer service. It's not an end in and of itself," Kelleher says.[13]

Back-office managers are encouraged to spend a day doing front-line jobs, such as working the gate or ticket counter, to hear customer issues firsthand and help solve recurring problems. In an article he wrote for the Peter F. Drucker Foundation in 1997, Kelleher described the company's marketing strategy: "We market ourselves based on the personality and spirit of ourselves. That sounds like an easy claim, but, in fact, it is a supremely dangerous position to stake out because if you're wrong, customers will let you know—with a vengeance. Customers are like a force of nature: You can't fool them, and you ignore them at your own peril."[14]

Even though the company has created customer evangelists partly because of its emphasis on creating a dialogue with them, it does not accept e-mail. A page on the company's Web site explains: "Call us traditional, but we elect to steer clear of the chat-style, respond-on-demand, quick casual format and focus on meaningful customer dialogue. This is not because we don't care. It's because that style counters our 30-plus year commitment to customer service. Our customers deserve accurate, specific, personal, and professionally written answers, and it takes time to research, investigate, and compose a real business letter. We answer every letter we receive in the order it arrives, and we streamline in order to keep our costs low, our people productive, our operating efficiency high, and our responses warm and personal."[15]

Arriving in that mailbag each month are requests from cities that the airline establish service in their airports. The requests pour in year after year, but Southwest prides itself on slow, continuous growth and a culture of maintaining low expectations. Because the company encourages and receives so much customer feedback, the prevailing attitude toward focus groups is pretty clear. "Why the hell should I spend money on focus groups?" Barrett asks. "I read every letter customers write."[16]

The company avoids most traditional forms of long-range planning and instead favors an integrated, customer-focused plan that incorporates societal trends and how Southwest intends to fit within that trend. Many people outside Southwest's executive circle are involved in this process.

Rich Marcotte is the mayor of Southwest Airlines. For nine years, he was Southwest's most frequent flyer out of Chicago, traveling at least 200 times a year while he was national marketing director for USA Tax Help in the 1990s. His typical schedule was to board a flight on a Sunday and fly to one of 20 client cities; return Tuesday night; fly again on Wednesday night to another client city; return Friday. Until 2001, he did this every week for nine years.

Along the way, Marcotte was nicknamed the "Mayor of Southwest" by the wife of a frequent-flyer rival. She joked about Marcotte's mayorlike persona in Southwest's gate areas. Although he doesn't fly as much for his new job, Marcotte still works each gate like a local politico, shaking hands, talking up business, professing a love for "his" airline, and pulling angry or frustrated travelers aside and calming them down. He signs up fellow passengers for Rapid Rewards, the company's frequent-flier program. Marcotte is a volunteer ambassador and salesperson for a company he describes as "family."

"It was a crazy schedule I had, but I enjoyed it because of Southwest," Marcotte says. "It's easy to tell friends and associates about something when you feel passionate about it. I've never seen an organization like it.

"I was treated like royalty."[17]

Because he was the company's best customer in the Midwest and because he got along with Southwest's Chicago team so well, the company treated him well outside the terminal. They gave him tickets to the NBA finals when Michael Jordan was the king of Chicago.

They gave him the opportunity to throw out the first pitch at a Chicago Cubs game, as shown in Figure 13.1. Southwest's regional marketing director, Patty Kryscha, ensured that Marcotte had a chance

Figure 13.1 | Flyer Marcotte Throwing a Strike at a Chicago Cubs Game

Rich Marcotte throws a strike at a Chicago Cubs game at Wrigley Field. Arranged for his behalf by Southwest's regional marketing director, throwing out the first pitch of a game was one of the many benefits Marcotte enjoyed by being one of Southwest's best customers and most prolific evangelists.

to meet his hero, Herb Kelleher. Marcotte estimates that at 200 trips per year for nine years and evangelizing Southwest to several people per trip, he's probably directly influenced at least 9,000 customers for the company. He's even volunteered to go out on the speaking circuit and address audiences on behalf of the airline if he was needed.

Said Parker of the company's customer evangelists: "The reason we have loyal customers is they've been touched by a Southwest Airlines employee."[18]

Patty Kryscha doesn't have a long white beard, red suit, or reindeer sleigh. But she could be easily mistaken for the female version of Kris Kringle; she even has a jolly laugh.

Kryscha is regional director of Southwest's Chicago field marketing office. Her job is to be the company's ambassador and develop relationships with the communities in Chicago, Indianapolis, Nashville, and Columbus by doling out gifts on behalf of Southwest Airlines. With her trove of plane tickets and gift certificates, and a modest marketing budget, Kryscha and her six-person team sort through 550 requests every year from local organizations, deciding who's naughty and who's nice.

In 2001, the Chicago field office donated 136 tickets to the local chapter of 67 different organizations, such as Big Brothers/Big Sisters, the YMCA, and the American Diabetes Association. Kryscha's office also donated 280 gift certificates ranging from $25 to $400 to groups such as the San Miguel School, the Blue Island Police Department, and the Mount Greenwood Little League.

United and American Airlines tend to sponsor symphonies and arts events, whereas Southwest typically supports good old-fashioned professional sports. Southwest has been involved with the Chicago Cubs since the company started service in Chicago in 1985. Kryscha says the partnership makes perfect sense because "Southwest is fun and the Cubs are fun."[19] The company's most frequent flyers are often invited to party with Kryscha and her crew at Wrigley Field, sometimes offering customers other than Rich Marcotte the chance to throw out the first pitch at games. "People here are passionate about the Cubs," Kryscha says, "so there is some transference."

But don't think that playing the role of Kringle is easy. "We get requests from so many deserving nonprofit organizations [for tickets or sponsorships]," Kryscha says. "The challenge is trying to decide who needs our help the most."[20] But that doesn't stop some of the "bleacher bums" from getting creative with their requests, like the group of fraternity brothers who called to ask Kryscha to comp the group's annual beer blast to New Orleans for Mardi Gras. It was for a good cause, they said, and they might raise a little bit of money, too. That got the naughty stamp. Kryscha and her team donate more than company freebies. Many times after work or during weekends they are volunteering for many of the local causes they believe in. They also consult with nonprofits on employee relations, serve on the boards of social services agencies, and mentor children through the YMCA. "Southwest encourages us to get involved," she says. "It's nice to have the freedom and flexibility to do that."[21]

Evangelism Scorecard: Southwest Airlines

Customer Plus-Delta

- Kelleher set the tone for executives to fly as passengers to get firsthand customer feedback.

- The company encourages customers to write and acknowledges every note with a handwritten response.

- Back-office managers are encouraged to work frontline jobs to hear directly from customers.

Build the Buzz

- Quirky and fun flight attendants get customers talking.

- Employees are encouraged to show their personality.

- Pay attention to detail; always call people back and bestow smiles.

Create Community

- Local field offices develop personal relationships with top local customers.

- Local field offices get involved in supporting community causes.

- Southwest supports employees' personal involvement in community causes.

Bite-Size Chunks

- Southwest initiated a "Friends Fly Free" promotion.

- It has holiday sales to encourage people to fly.

Create a Cause

- Southwest's cause is freedom—company strategy follows its cause, not the other way around.

- Employees and customers understand what the company stands for.

CHAPTER FOURTEEN

IBM: The Billion-Dollar Cause

To be honest, we'd open source just about anything the [Linux] community wanted.[1]

—Irving Wladawsky-Berger, vice president of technology strategy, IBM

A wave called Linux is heading toward the shoreline of computer operating system supremacy, and IBM is doing its best to ride it. Yes, stodgy, old-fashioned IBM.

In 2000, Big Blue committed $1 billion to help make Linux the most powerful free agent in the computer industry. Linux is a computer operating system that isn't controlled by Microsoft, Apple, or any other computer company. The character and personality of Linux is determined by a "gated community" of programmers who, while working at varying companies, volunteer their time to continually improve the operating system; they collaborate on writing the software so that it will run any computer. Companies like IBM package Linux on their various computers with accompanying software. The core version of Linux is free; companies that repackage it and add new features to it may charge money for it, but the cost is usually nominal. Very often, the operating system for some companies is a free tool for which they sell consulting services around. Microsoft controls the majority of operating systems with its own software, which it spends hundreds of millions of dollars developing, and earns even more from selling. Linux, which lies at the heart of what's known as the open source software movement, makes Microsoft very nervous. Linus Torvalds is the creator of Linux. In 1991, he set out to learn more about the Intel 386 processor; Torvalds was a student at the University of Helsinki in Finland, and he first announced his work that year by posting a message to a computer bulletin board: "I'm doing a (free) operating system (just a hobby, won't be big and professional like gnu) for 386 (486) AT clones. This has been brewing since April, and is starting to get ready. I'd like any feedback on things people like/dislike in minix, as my OS resembles it somewhat (same physical layout of the file-system (due to practical reasons among other things)."[2] Torvalds's post caught the attention of other programmers, and within a few years he had a small army of volunteers from around the world who provided feedback and wrote components of what he eventually called Linux, a play on his name and the Unix operating system. The irony, of course, is that Linux did turn out to be big and more than a hobby for him and thousands of people.

The growth of Linux has been a grassroots phenomenon. Because Linux doesn't require expensive licensing issues like proprietary computer operating systems and the software continues to grow and evolve based on the needs of its users, it was almost inevitable that Linux would become as popular as it has. When IBM invested $1 billion to make Linux part of its core strategy, that added a significant level of legitimacy to Linux and the notion of open source software. With its billion dollars, IBM financed the creation of Linux development centers around the world, training sales, marketing, and professional services experts to evangelize Linux to customers and developers. IBM gave $40 million worth of Linux software tools to software developers to create Linux applications. It redirected 2,000 IBM programmers to develop Linux versions of the company's entire suite of software products. But when it comes to Linux, the open source community sets the rules and agenda, not IBM.

To be in synch with its investment, IBM configured its entire vast line of servers—the computers that store and serve files, programs, and data—to run Linux. These include everything from the company's $1,500 Internet servers to its $3 million mainframes. The company is incorporating Linux into its other lines, too: Intel servers, Power-based servers, iSeries, storage, OEM (original equipment manufacturer) technology, and everything in its $9 billion software group. In 2005, the company invested $100 million specifically to broaden the use of Linux technologies within its Workplace product family and assist customers in constructing end-to-end Linux-based solutions that fit a variety of devices.[3] It had recognized the value of the contributed labor of Linux development as well as the grassroots, community-driven initiative for which tens of thousands of stakeholders would applaud the company and work harder to ensure the value of IBM's investment.

As in most revolutions in history, one man led the charge. In this case, the leader within the largest technology company in the world was Irving Wladawsky-Berger. The Cuban-born Wladawsky-Berger, who has a PhD in physics, led IBM's bold bet. His Linux strategy was more reminiscent of the entrepreneurial spirit of Silicon Valley than anything in IBM history. Wladawksy-Berger is a lifelong IBMer who began his career in IBM's research labs, consistently putting him on the leading edge of the company's technology efforts. In the 1980s, he was responsible for IBM's supercomputer efforts; in the mid-1990s, he was tasked with bringing the company into the age of the Internet.

The idea of IBM creating customer evangelists may seem like a stretch for a company whose history was not always customer-friendly. IBM was declared a monopolist by the federal government in 1969, and IBM of the 1970s was like Microsoft of the 1990s: It exerted vast amounts of control, power, and influence but never enjoyed the cult-like devotion of an Apple Computer. The old saying that "no one was ever fired for hiring IBM" was true because few alternatives existed. But in the early years of the 21st century, IBM's storyline began to change. Its embrace of an open source computer operating system is remarkable. Linux is the embodiment of what a community of like-minded and passionate individuals can achieve when they band together. Among the community of several hundred thousand developers IBM was courting, it had created a new class of customer evangelists previously unknown to the company because (1) it embraced a cause as much as a technology, (2) it lent support and credibility to a community, and (3) it made significant portions of its intellectual property freely available. In announcing the company's $1 billion investment during the eBusiness Conference and Expo in 2000, then IBM chief executive Lou Gerstner said IBM "is convinced that Linux can do for business applications what the Internet did for networking and communications."[4] By following the open standards and collaboration that fueled the development and rapid growth of the Internet, IBM will do the same with Linux and open source software.

But what is open source software, anyway? Eric S. Raymond documents its brief but influential history in the book *The Cathedral & the Bazaar*. He writes that Linux was the first project "for which a conscious and successful effort to use the entire world as its talent pool was made."[5] Open source software is akin to a local barn raising or a Habitat for Humanity home-building project: Like-minded people who may or may not know one another organize under a common goal to build something that will benefit a group of individuals and the community at large. The source of the software—the code that powers it—is open and available for anyone in the community to examine. By its nature, open source software is typically free or very inexpensive. It's that global talent pool and its key influencers whom IBM is courting. Some are responsible for purchasing hardware and software, whereas others recommend what to buy.

Courting the open source community made good business sense, too. According to International Data Corporation (IDC), Linux commanded 25 percent of the server market in 2004. The research firm expects revenue of servers, desktops, and packaged software running

Linux to exceed $35.7 billion by 2008. How big, then, was the community that IBM was courting?

"No one has done census work on this," says Jeff "Hemos" Bates, the executive editor of online technology community *slashdot.org*. He says that estimates are somewhere in the hundreds of thousands. "Welcome to the glory of counting."[6] How are some of the leaders of the open source community reacting to IBM's efforts? "IBM has done far more and made a greater investment in Linux than any other major vendor," concludes IDC analyst Dan Kusnetzky.[7]

IBM launched its Linux strategy with an iconic campaign using the symbols of peace, love, and a penguin. The penguin is the symbol for Linux; Torvalds selected it because the flightless birds are usually considered "cute, cuddly, and contented" but can also charge at an unwary visitor at what seems to be "100 mph." IBM even went so far as to announce its strategy in a rather uncharacteristic fashion. IBM's ad agency was supposed to have stenciled the three icons at busy intersections using biodegradable chalk but somehow the agency ended up using permanent spray paint. IBM claimed ignorance of the effort and paid fines to clean up the graffiti, but the publicity surrounding the stunts proved to be invaluable and showed a rebellious side to Big Blue. There was little ambiguity that IBM stood behind Linux in a new and offbeat way.

"We are members of an industry that's out to change the world," Wladawsky-Berger told *Linux Magazine*.

At the 2001 LinuxWorld Conference and Expo, then–IBM president Sam Palmisano (later promoted to chief executive officer) underscored the company's courting of the Linux community in the hope of making it evangelists. "Change—some are excited about it, some really threatened about it," he said, making not-so-sly references to Microsoft and Sun, which have held very public contempt for Linux. "You are the community that will get this done. But we need to work together."[8]

That encouragement means constant courting of a community loosely organized around belief in the ideals of a cooperative. As

Figure 14.1 | IBM's Campaign to Launch Linux Support

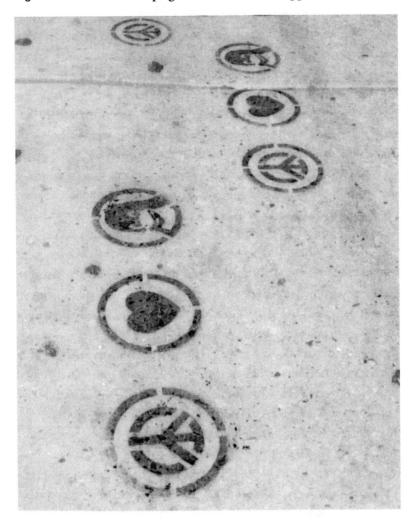

IBM's marketing campaign to launch its Linux initiative highlighted Peace/ Love/Penguin logos that were spray painted on city sidewalks around the country. Although some municipalities were not amused by the stunt and subsequently fined IBM and its marketing agency, the campaign garnered plenty of publicity and probably helped the company's overall "street credibility."[9]

explained by Tim O'Reilly, founder and president of O'Reilly & Associates and widely considered one of the leaders of the open source community: "Open source is really a gift culture in which you gain status by what you give away."[10]

Even though IBM is making inroads, hurdles remain. It rankled some to hear IBM's Linux evangelist Wladawsky-Berger say: "The more we encourage the development of Linux, the more it will drive our business."[11]

"The comments that IBM has made that their support for Linux is predicated on not just a belief in open source, but that it will help their business, to my mind means they are not changing their DNA," says *slashdot.org*'s Bates. "They are finding that they can be a better business by supporting Linux, and that's not changing your DNA—that's being a smarter business, and I think IBM deserves support for that."[12]

But O'Reilly insists that IBM has so far made the right moves.

"I thought IBM did a great job out of the gate," O'Reilly said. "They quickly organized a tiger team to look into it, flew a bunch of outsiders in to brief their team, and formulated a policy. There are always skeptics, but in general I'd say that IBM has done a better job than most of the big companies at getting the open source community on its side. It's made real contributions to a number of projects, not just lip service."[13]

The technology community message boards are showing some increasing support as well. "Top marks to Big Blue for doing the right thing," says one member of *slashdot.org*.[14] "I applaud IBM for the fantastic software support of Linux. Not only for porting more apps to Linux but developing new ones altogether on the platform," says a member of the Temple of the Screaming Penguin, another technology site.[15]

Indeed, it is IBM's willingness to talk openly about the potential of Linux to help its business and the community that is winning fans. Says Intel's Dawn Foster, who pens the *Open Culture* blog: "IBM has been absolutely brilliant in their participation . . . within open source communities partly because they have been so up-front about their financial motivations. The open source community values honesty and transparency, and by not hiding their motivations, people have a better understanding of why IBM takes certain actions. IBM's large contributions (in code, developers, and more) have also made them popular with open source communities. More companies should learn from IBM's successes."[16]

Wladawsky-Berger regularly surveys the technology community to gauge its needs. His team has talked to thousands of developers, asking them how IBM can support them while simultaneously encouraging them to develop Linux-based programs. It initially built its Linux strategy by surveying 2,700 customers, asking what they found appealing about Linux and where they're heading in the future. Guy Kawasaki, CEO of Garage Technology Ventures, loves this idea. "There's a fascination to how IBM can be evangelistic with Linux," he says.[17]

The irony is not lost on Wladawsky-Berger. As he told *Business 2.0* in 2001: "The Internet and Linux are far bigger than IBM."[18] He speaks reverently of the Linux community; in interviews, he often defers to "the community" before formulating major strategic decisions. Prior to 1990, when IBM controlled the vast majority of computer operating systems, that would have been heresy, and programmers know it. IBM's change of heart has been consistently winning over the technology community, primarily because it has decided to trust the community to develop the core operating system.

"There is a very long tradition of researchers writing papers and publishing them openly," he says. "Their peers then read the papers, write additional papers on the topic, and everybody builds on everybody else's ideas. The sharing of this information, whether you're in a university, a research lab, or the private sector, is what advances research and innovation for the benefit of your community.[19]

"To be honest, we'd open source just about anything the [Linux] community wanted."[20]

With its Linux initiative, IBM is trying to build on that idea and avoid the traps other technology companies fall into of thinking they know what's best for the customer or that technology customers don't know what to ask for if it hasn't been invented yet.

"IBM remains the most seriously committed vendor in the field around Linux," Gartner analyst George Weiss said in 2000. "They have the most to win, as well as the most to lose."[21]

IBM is expanding its support of open source beyond Linux. The company has offered up 500 patents to the open source community. The patents will be open for use by any individual, company, or community to use in software that will be open source by the standards of the Open Source Initiative (OSI). According to one report, IBM theorizes the initial pledge of patents will help form a "patent commons" where technology companies release some privately held patents to foster innovation that would benefit the larger community.[22] In August 2006, the company announced it would focus its open-source efforts in eight additional areas that affect a large part of its core businesses. "IBM is going to be as bold and aggressive with open source as we are with Linux . . . more broadly transforming our company with the open movement," said Scott Handy, IBM vice president of Linux and open source.[23]

The billion-dollar bet in Linux appeared to be paying off. In 2004, IBM reported double-digit growth among customers that deployed the company's Workplace collaboration software on Linux.[21]

Evangelism Scorecard: IBM

Customer Plus-Delta

- Wladawsky-Berger spends most of his time visiting customers around the world.

Napsterize Your Knowledge

- IBM is making $40 million worth of software tools available for free to spur the development of additional Linux applications.

Build the Buzz

- IBM's bold program—$1 billion for promoting open source—created waves of buzz.

- "Peace/Love/Linux" guerilla marketing campaign made news for its hipness.

Create Community

- IBM is building goodwill among the existing community of open source developers by speaking at its conferences, providing tools, building information-packed Web sites for developers, and sending e-mail newsletters.

Bite-Size Chunks

- A number of IBM-created programs are free and available for downloading.

Create a Cause

- By throwing its considerable weight and influence behind Linux, IBM joins the open source movement.

CHAPTER FIFTEEN

Customer Evangelism Workshop

In the arena of human life the honors and rewards fall to those who show their good qualities in action.

—Aristotle

Creating customer evangelists requires planning, resources, and patience. The six tenets provide a framework to plan your evangelism strategies and tactics. They are not steps to be performed in a specific order; rather, they are concepts to consider as your customer evangelism grows and matures. To review, the tenets are:

- Customer Plus-Delta. Continuously understanding what your customers love about you and what they would like to see improved.

- Napsterize your knowledge. Sharing your intellectual capital in ways that are easily passed on to others.

- Build the buzz. Using natural networks that exist to get people talking.

- Create community. Finding ways to create a sense of belonging among your customers.

- Bite-size chunks. Developing easily digestible pieces for new evangelists.

- Create a cause. Rallying customers around something bigger than you.

In our case-study companies, the tenets are applied differently. The Evangelism Scorecard at the end of each case-story chapter provides ideas on how to apply the tenets to your business. To think about this further, we have developed a series of questions to consider for each tenet.

Customer Plus-Delta

This is the first tenet because it's the most important. It's fundamental to any evangelism strategy. Ask your current customers this series of open-ended questions to uncover more about who they are, how they feel about their relationship with you and your organization, and how they perceive the quality and value of your products and services. We suggest that the era of exceedingly long and complex surveys is over. Short, conclusive surveys are the best tool for gathering data and feedback from busy and influential people who spread the most buzz. In fact, we suggest just one primary question whose answer becomes the determinant for several follow-up questions. The fundamental question is:

- *Do your recommend our product, brand, or company to friends, colleagues, or family members?* We suggest multiple-choice answers of "Yes," "No," or "Don't know." (You can create an aggregate customer evangelism score by subtracting every "No" and "Don't know" from the total sum of "Yes" responses.)

- If the answer is "yes": *How often? In what forums?* Find out who your evangelists really are. Pay special attention to them— they are key to recruiting new customers. You could also ask after getting a "yes" what they love specifically about your product, brand, or company. You may be able to capture a few testimonials for your use. You may also want to know what do customers say *specifically* when they make a recommendation. Pay close attention to the wording they use to describe you and why others should buy your product or service. This input can help refine your marketing communications. A "yes" is also a good opportunity to find out what customers value most about your company, product, or brand. You may think it's the latest feature added to your product, but customers may say it's your telephone support. Ask customers to quantify the value of your products and services using real measures, if possible.

- If the answer is "no" or "don't know": *What do customers say you should specifically improve or change to earn a recommendation?* Customers evangelize products they feel are worthy to refer to friends and family. If you hear many negative answers to this question, perhaps a product overhaul is in order before continuing with your customer evangelism efforts. A "no" or "don't know" is a good opportunity to reach out to a customer who's fallen through your company's cracks, been the victim of a product defect, or had the misfortune to deal with an employee who was having a bad day. Often what these customers wish for most of all is a simple apology.

- Finally, do you provide simple and systematic ways for your customers to regularly provide feedback? Does your Web site make it easy for customers to enter suggestions for all areas of your business? Formally surveying your customers at regular intervals is good, but allowing customers to provide you with ongoing feedback is better.

Napsterize Your Knowledge

Napsterize parts of your organization, such as sharing intellectual capital and processes, to make them more valuable. Napsterize the obvious parts of your business that improve customer interaction or real-time data. Focus on innovating existing products and services that could become co-opted by Napsterization or commoditization.

- How can you become an information resource in your industry? How can you externalize internal company knowledge and expertise?

- Can you write an article on how to select a company like yours? Position your company as one that is looking out for its customers' best interests by helping them with the selection process instead of one that just wants to hand out its brochure.

- Can you fill your Web site with articles, book reviews, links to other resources, events lists, and so on, pertaining to your specialty? Invite others to submit their suggestions for these things so you can post them for the good of the community.

- Can you package your knowledge to make it easily distributed?

For today's knowledge workers in industries such as consulting and technology, intellectual capital can be the company's most important asset. Keeping all expertise and knowledge bottled up inside the company doesn't help customers understand and spread the word about your core offerings.

Build the Buzz

Get people talking by creating buzz about your products and services. Leverage the natural networks in society and business to break through the clutter with infectious word of mouth.

- Do you know what the current buzz is regarding your products and services? Search the Internet, especially newsgroups and chat rooms, to see what people are saying.

- Can you identify the network hubs and megahubs for your industry? How many of these people do you have an existing relationship with?

- Are you nurturing relationships with these influencers? Do you offer them special access to your company? Do you feed them information about new products and services? Do you solicit their input?

- What is it about your product that's different? How can you make it stand out? Is there a story associated with your product?

- Are you selling products or experiences? Can you design a customer experience that will get people talking?

Create Community

Help customers bond with you and each other by adding community programs to your marketing. Your current customer evangelists will help recruit new members into the community.

- Are customers already calling you to ask how they can meet other customers like themselves? Are customers already connecting to each other without you, via the Web perhaps?

- Ask customers to help develop a community program. Solicit their input and watch for the individuals who are eager to help.

Can you appoint one as a leader of a specific program in your community-building efforts?

- Just try it and see what happens. Gather feedback from participants (and nonparticipants) all along the way. Let them shape your community program so that it provides value for all involved. Don't be afraid to end it if it's just not working.

- Can you hold a fun event to bring customers together to swap stories with other customers, à la eBay Live or Harley Owner Group rallies?

- Add community features, such as online bulletin boards, to your Web site. Create and moderate an e-mail discussion group to get customers to connect. Start a blog to facilitate a conversation with your customers.

- Put a human face on your marketing. Feature your current evangelistic customers in your marketing communications efforts. Solicit testimonials and sprinkle them liberally throughout your Web site, brochures, and advertising.

- Create a special community program for your most evangelistic fans. Make them feel as though they are part of a select few who receive special benefits. Give these special few all the materials they need to spread the word for you. Embrace fan sites if you are lucky enough to have them.

Bite-Size Chunks

Break up your product or service portfolio into bite-size chunks, which introduces your company's products and services with small, easily consumed pieces. This strategy puts more of your product into the marketplace for people to experience and evangelize.

- For consumer commodities, give out samples of your products to network hubs. Ask them to introduce you to other network hubs to share samples with. Find communities where prospective customers gather and supply samples liberally.

- For technology products, can you offer a limited-time or limited-capacity trial version to prospective customers?

- For services companies, can you offer a "starter" version of service? Divide up your service portfolio into chunks that customers can bite off, one at a time.

Create a Cause

To show the world what you are really about, create a cause for your company. A good cause is meaningful; it is something that people—customers and employees—can believe in and rally around. When people believe in your cause, they'll evangelize you to others and recruit new believers into the fold. A cause need not be a charity to which you donate time or services; a cause can be a point around which your customers and employees rally—they support it and believe in it. Southwest Airlines and Harley-Davidson have built their company cultures and marketing strategies around the idea of freedom. No customer ever rallied for a company cause built around the notion of increased shareholder return.

- Does a societal issue affect significant numbers of your customers? What can you do to support a charitable cause that addresses it?

- Instead of just selling products, sell a dream. Think bigger about what would improve customers' lives, what would change your customers' world. Challenge yourself and your organization to think big and create a message of inspiration.

We've come to the end of this book, but we hope this is the beginning of a relationship. Our objective was to outline the six tenets of customer evangelism and help you think about customers and marketing in a new light, with a new (or reinforced) theology. The case-study companies inspired us to write this book; we hope they inspire you to action. Let us know how you are creating customer evangelists. Do you have a story about how you are doing this? Have you applied an idea from the book that was successful? Do you have some ideas to share with others? Join our customer evangelism community at *www.ChurchoftheCustomer.com.*

Creating Customer Vigilantes

If customers consider your communication with them like receiving personal letters from a friend, you are on the right path. Because of its relative low cost and ease of use, e-mail marketing communications are also misused and abused. Too often, companies view e-mail as a customer *acquisition* tool, but it's not. It's a customer *retention* tool. Yet the siren's song of e-mail marketers who promise untapped gold at the end of the Internet rainbow wails louder and louder. A client of ours received an unsolicited commercial e-mail about a broadcast e-mail program that promised to help them land new customers. Our client asked for advice: Should she take the offer or reject it? The company's pitch resonated like a beacon of possibility:

If you send a Broadcast Email Advertisement to 50,000,000 People and Just 1 of 5,000 People Respond, You Can Generate 10,000 EXTRA ORDERS! How Much EXTRA PROFIT is this for You?

The pitch even calculated the math:

Let's say you . . . Sell a $24.95 PRODUCT or SERVICE. Let's say you . . . Receive JUST 1 ORDER for EVERY 2,500 EMAILS.

CALCULATION OF YOUR EARNINGS BASED ON
THE ABOVE STATISTICS:
[Day 1]: $4,990 [Week 1]: $34,930 [Month 1]: $139,720

Research from analyst firms such as Forrester, Jupiter, and eMarketer all tout e-mail marketing as a cost-effective way to reach customers. Like most offers that arrive unsolicited, this one is too good to be true. This is not legitimate e-mail marketing. It's spam. Spammer companies like the one mentioned above and their unwitting customers create "badwill." They erode the overall effectiveness of customercentric e-mail communications. Worse, spam creates the antithesis of the customer evangelist: the vigilante customer, who actively campaigns against you.

As a business owner or executive considering unsolicited broadcast e-mail as a marketing tactic, you can expect all sorts of results, and none includes easy money. You may instantly anger a group of quite vocal activists. You may raise the ire of vigilantes who publicly try to shame or embarrass you. Send an unsolicited commercial e-mail to a prospect without permission and you risk having that person angrily call your business, flood your inbox with hateful and vengeful responses, and report your company to the Federal Trade Commission. You risk tarnishing your name. In addition to bothering you at work, the vigilante may encourage others to do the same. The vigilante may append your company's name to online lists of "known spammers." People who didn't even receive your broadcast e-mail may send you angry e-mail, postal mail, and phone calls. You may lose your e-mail services. Sending spam through your Internet service provider (ISP) may cost you your Internet service. Spam clogs e-mail servers, sometimes crashes them, and otherwise causes headaches and complaints for an ISP. Your ISP may dump you rather than contend with those headaches. You will have wasted your time chasing ghosts. Some companies promise millions of e-mail addresses for your use. You may as well write made-up names and addresses on envelopes and send those through the U.S. Postal Service because it's the same principle. Most of the "millions" of e-mail addresses promised by spam merchants are computer-generated guesses based on deduction theory: *ben@aol.com, ben1@aol.com, ben2@aol.com,* and on into digital infinity.

That said, there are ways to grow your business and create customer evangelists through effective e-mail marketing:

1. Focus on building your own in-house e-mail list. If you offer different and unique products, create lists for each product.

2. Always request permission to send people e-mail. Always.

3. Make your e-mail communications relevant and anticipated. Tell people what they can expect from you.

4. Offer something of value. Offer a free white paper, product sample, hints and tips, etc.

5. Provide relevant content on an ongoing basis to a third party source. Is there a professional organization in your industry with a newsletter that your potential customers read? If your company provides IT consulting services, for instance, write a 250–500 word article for an association's monthly e-mail newsletter that goes out to 10,000 subscribers. The true path to customer evangelism is paved with goodwill, and it never includes spam.

Creating something that spreads

When customers evangelize you to their friends and colleagues, what they say is as important as the passion behind their words. In short, are your evangelists pitching what you want prospects to hear? To make it easy for customers to describe what you do, they must understand the idea of your company and be able to easily spread that idea to others. An ideavirus creates buzz, which contributes to the contagion of creating customer evangelists. For an idea to spread, it must be easy for you to remember because then it will be easier for others to remember. It's the equivalent of the elevator pitch, or what you would say to a stranger about your value proposition (or someone else's) during the time it takes to ride 20 floors in an elevator. It's roughly equal to the attention span of most prospective customers in generating an interest in your product or service.

To create effective customer evangelists, your customers must know your elevator pitch as well as you do. How smooth is your company's pitch? Do people you meet nod knowingly when you describe your company's products or services, or do they look puzzled and ask you to explain more? ABC Technology Services (not the company's real name) asked for our advice in landing new clients. Company executives described themselves approximately this way: "ABC designs and delivers network and systems management solutions that assist companies in cost-effectively maximizing the performance, uptime, and availability of their network infrastructures." Not very easy to remember, even for them. They struggled with that for about 15 minutes. Here's the advice we gave them:

1. Interview ten current customers and ask them to describe what ABC does and the value it delivers. By now you probably realize that what customers say is integral to helping people spread the word. It became clear that ABC's customers engaged the company during periods of crisis: computer systems were slow, e-mail was malfunctioning, or employees had to frequently reboot computers. ABC promptly fixed these problems and installed monitoring software to make sure these issues were history, not current events.

2. Use the words of customers to reframe the pitch. In this case, it was to focus on the pain felt by prospective customers. Because ABC's primary source of leads was via word of mouth, we suggested a casual tone. Instead of "network and systems

management," we suggested "You know how when y[...]
work, and you are pulling your hair out because of com[...]
problems? Your system is slow, you can't send or receive e-m[...]
or you have to reboot your computer a lot? Well, we fix those
problems." Since their customers were decidedly non-technical
we suggested they avoid all techie-talk in favor of simple language and a context that prospects could identify with: pain.

3. The ABC executives tried the new pitch at a networking
   event. They were amazed at the profuse head-nodding when
   delivering their new pitch. A failing computer system is simple to understand because it's experienced by almost everyone. That makes it easy for someone to tell others, as we saw
   demonstrated several times at the event. ABC landed six leads
   from this one event alone using their new and improved
   pitch. Here's a simple, step-by-step process to better understand how to talk about your business, product, or brand:

   1. Interview (or have a third party interview) your current
      satisfied customers.

   2. Ask the customers to describe any pains or needs that first
      motivated them to buy your product or service.

   3. Ask the customers to describe the value of your products
      or services.

   4. Ask the customers how they would evangelize your busi-
      ness to others.

   5. Write down exactly—word for word—the answers to these
      questions.

   6. Reframe your pitch using the pain points of how cus-
      tomers would describe your services to others.

   7. Test and refine your pitch at networking events.

ned pitch in other marketing materials, such
site or brochures.

ng Customer Evangelism

Marketers struggle constantly with measuring the success of customer programs. To paraphrase the old adage by department store magnate John Wanamaker, "I know 50 percent of my marketing efforts are working. I just don't know which 50 percent." It's challenging, but not impossible. And the Internet constantly offers new measurement tools and tactics. Our research has shown that customer evangelism marketing strategies improve customer loyalty and increase revenue from current customers. When organizations focus on customer relationships, they tend to build more loyal customers who purchase more frequently, and sometimes exclusively. Customer evangelism can reduce customer acquisition costs because current, evangelistic customers recruit new customers on behalf of organizations they believe in.

To create metrics of success, first establish your current benchmarks:

- Number of current customers

- Customer retention rate (%)

- Revenue from repeat purchases of current customers

Measure these goals quarterly or annually. They are your big-picture organizational goals. To measure success among the six tenets of customer evangelism on a weekly, monthly, or quarterly basis, try these metrics.

1. Customer Plus-Delta (continuously gather customer feedback).

   - How many ideas for new products and services were gathered?

- How much revenue was generated by the new products and services?

- How many previously unknown problems were fixed based on customer feedback?

- How did the suggestions improve product quality?

- Did the suggestions help save money? If so, how much?

2. Napsterize your knowledge (share your knowledge freely).

   - In how many places on the Internet is your company's expertise mentioned?

   - In how many places online are your white papers posted?

   - How many articles did you publish or have published?

   - What is the referral or pass-along rate of your free e-mail newsletter?

3. Build the buzz (expertly tap into word-of-mouth networks).

   - How did new and prospective customers say they discovered you? Ask for the specific place, press mention, or person. If it was a personal referral, what did the referrer say?

   - Analyze traffic to your Web site. Which organizations visit the most?

   - What types of organizations are they?

   - Are they the ones you want visiting?

   - What part of the world are they from?

   - Which parts of the site do they visit most?

   - How are people discovering your site? Most Web site traffic analysis tools can measure search terms entered into search engines that brought visitors to your site.

4. Create community (encourage your customers to meet and share information).

   • How many customers are on your e-mail list?

   • How is your subscriber rate trending: increasing, decreasing, or flat?

   • How many customer events have you held? How many guests did customers bring? How many of those guests became customers?

5. Make bite-size chunks (devise specialized, smaller offerings to get customers to bite).

   • How many different product or service offerings make up your portfolio?

   • How many of those offerings have you divided into sample offerings?

   • How many prospects have sampled your product or service?

   • How many prospects turned into customers?

   • What's the referral rate of people who sampled your offering and told others?

6. Create a cause (focus on making the world, or an industry, better).

   • How many people contact you because they believe in your cause?

   • How many of them became customers?

   • How many customers say they purchase from you exclusively because of what you stand for?

   • How many people send their resumes asking to work in your organization because they believe in what you do or what you stand for?

Employ these metrics for several quarters or a year, then revisit the big-picture benchmark metrics and compare the previous numbers. If you have maintained a high level of quality and consistently execute well, your big-picture numbers should be at least 5 percent higher. If you believe in customer evangelism, then you probably steadfastly believe that doing the right thing for customers will pay dividends tenfold in the form of repeat purchases and customers who buy because of the word of others.

Spotting Evangelists in the Wild

No matter what, people talk about you. They talk about your company, your products and services, and your personality. Many say nice things, and some are absolutely gushy with their praise. Would you like to know who they are? How do you find your evangelists? It's almost too obvious to point out, but Google is one of the best tools available for small and medium businesses (or for the individual brand managers at big companies). Google makes it easy to know what's being said about anything with Google Alerts. It will discover where your product, company, or organization is mentioned and e-mail you whenever it finds a mention. Make note of everyone who compliments your products and services and everyone who criticizes them. For the people who love you, an e-mail or handwritten thank-you note is bound to build instant rapport. Inviting online fans to a special club with other evangelists for inside information about products and services is bound to create spirals of evangelism (and word of mouth—expect that everything you do will probably be talked about or blogged about). For those who take issue with your products or services, contacting them via e-mail or phone with a sympathetic ear can be a pivotal point for neutralizing a vigilante or perhaps even an evangelist. The difference between an unhappy customer and an evangelist is often just a phone call. More than anything, unhappy customers just want to be heard and acknowledged. Grant an unhappy customer that wish. For those who are vigilantes and wish to remain so, no matter what intervention you attempt, it's probably best to ignore them like a barking dog. They'll eventually tire themselves out.

To understand who is recommending you, ask prospective customers specifically how they discovered you. This is a fundamental step toward any evangelism. Know your evangelists by keeping detailed records of your referrers. If the referral was from a friend or colleague, ask the prospect for the name of the referrer. Keep detailed records of how people discovered you. One idea is to create a buzz map, which illustrates the actual routes of how they landed customers via word of mouth. A map of customer connections quickly illuminates your biggest evangelists.

If you have an opt-in e-mail list, add a field that asks how people discovered you. Continually refine the quantifiable nature of this field. You want to gather as much information as possible from this field, especially if the referrals are from people. Those are your evangelists!

Be an active participant in e-mail discussion lists and online bulletin boards that your customers frequent. Watch for customers who post recommendations about you. Cultivate relationships with them. Keep them in your loop. Use Web site tracking software to understand how Web site visitors discover you. If customers, prospects, fans, or evangelists link to your site, do not send them a cease-and-desist letter. This creates customer vigilantes, not customer evangelists. Do not let your corporate counsel argue that fan sites contribute to brand dilution. This is pure crap espoused by prosecutorial-minded lawyers intent on making customers play by ridiculous notions of trademark protection. (Note: Protect your trademarks against competitors, not customers.) Encourage links to your site, wherever fans would like to create them. Provide fans with pictures of your products, logos, movies, animations—anything that makes them feel connected to you. They are your volunteer sales force.

So you have spotted an evangelist who sings your praises to others. Now what? If strategy is also comprised of what not to do, here's

a story. In an online discussion forum in 2002, someone a
recommendation of a Web-based event registration service.
been pleased with the service we had used for hosting several eve
so we posted a complimentary recommendation to the forum. We
outlined the service's strong points and mentioned just one weak
point: no post-event reporting that outlines all fees deducted from
the total proceeds. The next day I received an e-mail from the director of product support at the registration company:

> "Jackie,
> Thanks for posting the nice message. We have earmarked
> several areas for improvement and are releasing a new version
> to the system soon that we think you will like very much. I did
> want to add something re: one comment . . . 'Only weak point:
> reports of actual transactions and fees is sparse.'
> I was surprised to see this. While we are aware of things we
> need to work on, reporting and revenue/transactional report-
> ing is extremely strong in our system. I just wanted to mention
> this, so you can be aware of these features before you use the sys-
> tem again. There are custom download functions that allow you
> to create your own download report formats. We have monthly
> revenue reports in simple format. There are downloadable reve-
> nue reports. Plus you can view and download detailed account-
> ing reports (with all line items included).
> Before you use the system next, feel free to set up an ap-
> pointment with me, and I'll walk you through these features. I
> think these will be of tremendous use."

I had evangelized this company's service to 3,300 people on an
e-mail discussion list. Instead of acknowledging that perhaps the design
of their system was flawed, he took issue with my comment, assumed
it was my error, and pressed me to get some training. In essence, he
said, "Thanks for saying nice things about us to a lot of people for free,
but get some training before you talk again about us." Of course, I no

npany. Why should I now? We'll stop short
ny name here.

five tips on what to do when you spot an

1. Contact the evangelist. Thank her profusely. If you don't personally know the person, call her. Find out more about her business, her challenges, and her personal interests.

2. If they say something you wish they hadn't, pick up the phone and call. If you only have an e-mail address, request a phone conversation. Be genuinely inquisitive in understanding their issues. Don't chastise customers for saying something you perceive to be wrong.

3. Put the person on your list of evangelists for a future opportunity to thank them in a more special way. A simple rule of thumb: Don't treat your customers like a socialist country where everyone is equally important. Your evangelists deserve special treatment. The best treatment is attention, not necessarily discounts or coupons.

4. Reward your evangelists unexpectedly. If your evangelists contact you to purchase additional products or services, provide extra value. Send a book. Hand them an extra set of football tickets. Introduce them to your CEO and/or president.

5. Develop a formal evangelist program that periodically rewards all of your evangelists. Host an annual party and invite only the evangelists. Take your best evangelists to lunch every quarter.

Remember, customer evangelism is a gift. It's true customer loyalty. Treat your evangelists like the royalty they are.

Chapter 1: A Customer Evangelism Manifesto

1. Southwest Airlines provided the authors with a packet of letters it received after September 11, 2001.

2. Ann McGee-Cooper, telephone interview with authors, 15 March 2002.

3. "The One Number You Need to Grow," *Harvard Business Review,* December 2003.

4. "Let's All Blame the Marketing Director," MP3 and lyrics on *Harpell.com: www.harpell.com/results.*

5. David Shenk, *Data Smog.* (San Francisco: Harper, 1997), 30.

6. This study is quoted in *The Influentials* by Ed Keller and Jon Berry. (New York: Free Press, 2003), 5.

7. This data is from BIGresearch's Simultaneous Media Usage Survey released in December, 2005.

8. Maxine Clark, telephone and e-mail interviews with authors, February–April 2002.

Chapter 2: When Customers Believe

1. Guy Kawasaki, interview with authors, Palo Alto, California, 2 February 2002.

2. Ibid.

3. Ibid.

4. George Silverman, *Secrets of Word-of-Mouth Marketing: How to Trigger Exponential Sales through Runaway Word of Mouth.* (New York: AMACOM, 2001), 15–16.

5. Kim Girard, "The Return of the Crummy Job," *Business 2.0*, 6 February 2001.

6. Tim Sanders, interview with authors, Chicago, 25 February 2002.

7. K.C. Swanson, "The Joy of Pepsi," *TheStreet.com*, 18 April 2001.

Chapter 3: Customer Plus-Delta

1. "Using Complaints for Quality Assurance Decisions," TARP, 1997. *www.e-satisfy.co.uk/research2.asp*

2. The Communispace June 2006 study is called "What Companies Gain From Listening: The Effect of Community Membership on Members' Attitudes and Behavior in Relation to the Sponsoring Company."

3. Jackie Sloan, telephone interview with authors, 2 April 2002.

4. Deborah Ball, "Toll-Free Tips: Nestle Hotlines Yield Big Ideas," *Wall Street Journal*, 3 September 2006.

5. Chicago Public Radio (WBEZ) research study, March 2002.

6. Michael Totty, "Information, Please: How three companies are using the Web to find out more about their customers—or to let their customers know more about them," *Wall Street Journal*, 29 October 2001.

7. Alex Johnston, telephone interview with authors, 2 April 2002.

8. Maxine Clark, telephone and e-mail interviews with authors, February–April 2002.

Chapter 4: Napsterize Your Knowledge

1. Stewart Brand, *The Media Lab: Inventing the Future at MIT.* (Viking Penguin, 1987).

2. Editorial, "Waiting to Be Napsterized?" *National Underwriter Life & Health/Financial Services Edition Online*, 5 February 2001. *www.nunews.com/lifeandhealth/editorials/020501/L200106waiting.asp*

3. Joel Selvin, "Did Napster Help Boost Record Sales?" *San Francisco Chronicle*, 5 August 2001.

4. Peter Rojas, "Fabulous Do-It-Yourself Manufacturing: Xerox never duplicated like this," *Red Herring*, 1 May 2001.

5. Massachusetts Institute of Technology, "MIT to Make Nearly All Course Materials Available Free on the World Wide Web," MIT press release, 4 April 2001. *web.mit.edu/newsoffice/nr/2001/ocw.html*

6. The information from Anne Margulies at MIT was compiled by listening to a recorded presentation she delivered to an audience of educators in Missouri in February 2006.

Chapter 5: Build the Buzz

1. Emanuel Rosen, interview with authors, Palo Alto, California, 6 February 2002.

2. Ibid.

3. "Cuban calls out NBA's director of officiating," *ESPN.com*, 7 January 2001. *espn.go.com/nba/news/2002/0107/1307127.html*

4. Mark Cuban, interview with authors, Dallas, 20 January 2002.

5. Ibid.

6. Gerry Khermouch, "Buzz Marketing," *BusinessWeek*, 30 July 2001. *www.businessweek.com/magazine/content/01_31/b3743001.htm*

7. John Gaffney, "The Cool Kids Are Doing It. Should You?" *Business 2.0*, October 2001. *www.business2.com/articles/mag/0,1640,17380,FF.html*

8. Emanuel Rosen, interview with authors, Palo Alto, California, 6 February 2002.

9. Joseph Pine II and James H. Gilmore, *The Experience Economy*. (Boston: Harvard Business School Press, 1999).

10. Ibid.

11. Renee Dye, "The Buzz on Buzz," *Harvard Business Review*, November–December 2000.

12. Tim Sanders, interview with authors, Chicago, 25 February 2002.

13. Richard Dawkins, *The Selfish Gene*. (Oxford University Press, 1990).

Chapter 6: Create Community

1. Daryl Urquhart, telephone interview with authors, 2 April 2002.

2. Bill Samuels Jr., interview with authors, 27 October 2005.

3. Ibid.

4. Ibid.

5. More on eBay live at *pages.ebay.com/ebaylive*

6. Red carpet photo at *www.flickr.com/photos/sculbers/172306926*

7. Erich Joachimsthaler and David Aaker, "Building Brands without Mass Media," *Harvard Business Review*, January–February issue, 1997.

8. Melanie Wells, "Cult Brands," *Forbes*, 16 April 2001.

9. Full Circle Consulting: *www.fullcirc.com*. Find the Online Facilitation e-mail discussion list at *groups.yahoo.com/group/onlinefacilitation*.

10. Lisa M. Bowman, "Warner Bros. Backs Off Harry Potter Fight," *News.com*, 16 March 2001.

11. Marc Weingaten, "LOTR: The Fellowship of the Web," *Business 2.0*, January 2002.

Chapter 7: Bite-Size Chunks

1. The Quotations Page: *www.quotationspage.com/quotes/Henry_Ford/*

2. Sampling statistics from James P. Santella & Associates: *www.santella.com/marketing.htm#RESULTS%20OF%20BRAND%20MARKETING%202001%20SURVEY*

3. Gerald Haman, interview with authors, Chicago, 12 October 2001.

4. Matt Fitzgerald, interview with authors, Dallas, 29 January 2002.

Chapter 8: Create a Cause

1. Guy Kawasaki, *Selling the Dream: How to Promote Your Product, Company, or Ideas—and Make a Difference—Using Everyday Evangelism.* (New York: Harper Business, 1992), 4.

2. Guy Kawasaki, interview with authors, Palo Alto, California, 2 February 2002.

3. Kawasaki, *Selling the Dream*, 14.

4. Richard Cross and Janet Smith, *Customer Bonding: 5 Steps to Lasting Customer Loyalty.* (Lincolnwood, IL: NTC Business Books, 1995), 95.

5. Sue Atkins, "The Wider Benefits of Backing a Good Cause," *Marketing*, 9 September 1999: *www.psaresearch.com/bib4314.html*

6. Business in the Community: *www.bitc.org.uk/marketing.html*

7. Carol Cone, "Cause Branding in the 21st Century," Public Service Advertising Research Center, 1998. *www.psaresearch.com/causebranding.html*

8. Harvey Meyer, "When the Cause Is Just," *Journal of Business Strategy*, November–December 1999. *www.psaresearch.com/bib4313.html*

9. Dan Pallotta, interview with authors, Los Angeles, 13 February 2002.

10. Brian Erwin, interview with authors, 22 March 2002.

11. Maxine Clark, "Putting the Heart Back in Retailing," *Texas A&M Retailing Issues Letter,* January 2001, Volume 13, Number 1.

Chapter 9: SolutionPeople: The High-Flying Solutionman

1. Gerald Haman, interviews with authors, Chicago, various dates, October 2001–May 2002.
2. Ibid.
3. Ibid.
4. Ibid.
5. Ibid.
6. Ibid.
7. Ibid.
8. Ibid.
9. Ibid.
10. Ibid.
11. Kevin Olsen, interview with authors, Downers Grove, Illinois, 12 March, 2002.
12. Ibid.
13. Haman, interview.

Chapter 10: O'Reilly Media: The History Lessons of O'Reilly's Wars

1. Tim O'Reilly, interview with authors, Sebastopol, California, 6 February, 2002.
2. Evelyn S. McClure, *Sebastopol, California: History, Homes, and People,* 1995, Belleview Press.
3. Simon Heseltine, "The Crimean War (1865-56)," *mo.essortment.com /thecrimeanwar_rezc.html.*
4. *tim.oreilly.com*
5. O'Reilly, interview.
6. *tim.oreilly.com*
7. O'Reilly, interview.
8. Ibid.
9. Ibid.
10. Sara Winge, interview with authors, Sebastopol, California, 7 February, 2002 and via e-mail, various dates.

11. O'Reilly, interview.
12. Ibid.
13. Ibid.
14. Ibid.
15. Jeff "Hemos" Bates, e-mail interview with authors, various dates, 25 March, 2002–15 April, 2002.
16. Brian Erwin, telephone interview with authors, 22 March, 2002.
17. Ibid.
18. O'Reilly, interview.
19. Ibid.
20. Erwin, interview.
21. Ibid.
22. Erwin, interview.
23. O'Reilly, interview.
24. Simone Paddock, telephone interview with authors, 10 August, 2001.
25. O'Reilly, interview.
26. Ibid.
27. Ibid.
28. Ibid.
29. Ibid.
30. Ibid.
31. Ibid.
32. Ibid.

Chapter 11: The Dallas Mavericks: The New Mavericks of Marketing

1. Mark Cuban, interviews with authors, Dallas, Texas, and via e-mail, various dates, 30 January, 2002–15 April 2002.
2. Jaime Aron, "Sweet Revenge: Billionaire Mavericks owner dishes ice cream," Associated Press, January 16, 2002.
3. Kevin B. Blackistone, "Calling a Bluff: What's Cuban's number?" *The Dallas Morning News,* January 19, 2002.
4. Cuban, interview.
5. Ibid.
6. Ibid.

7. Rick Alm, interview with authors, Dallas, Texas, 30 January, 2002.

8. Todd Walley, interview with authors, Dallas, Texas, 29 January, 2002.

9. Chris Bontrager, interview with authors, Dallas, Texas, 29 January, 2002.

10. George Killebrew, interview with authors, Dallas, Texas, 29 January, 2002.

11. Alm, interview.

12. Ibid.

13. Cuban, interview.

14. Ibid.

15. Ibid.

16. Ibid.

17. George Prokos, interview with authors, Dallas, Texas, 29 January, 2002.

18. Shawn Bradley, e-mail interview with authors, 17 April, 2002.

19. Greg Buckner, e-mail interview with authors, 17 April, 2002.

20. Cuban, interview.

21. Cuban, interview.

22. Matt Fitzgerald, interviews with authors, Dallas, Texas, via telephone and e-mail, various dates, 29 January, 2002–29 September 2006.

23. Ibid.

24. Ibid.

25. Ibid.

26. Ibid.

27. Cuban, interview.

28. Ibid.

29. Ibid.

30. Ibid.

31. Ibid.

32. Bradley, interview.

33. Buckner, interview.

34. Prokos, interview.

35. Cuban, interview.

Chapter 12: Build-A-Bear Workshop: A Bear Market for Retailing

1. Maxine Clark, interviews with authors via telephone and e-mail, various dates, 22 February, 2002–20 April, 2002.

2. Robert Berner, Gerry Khermouch and Aixa Pascual, "Retail Reckoning: There are just too many stores. Warning: Big shakeout ahead," *BusinessWeek*, December 10, 2001.

3. Cheryl Hall, "The Right Stuff: Creator of Build-A-Bear Workshop finds success by remaining a child at heart," *The Dallas Morning News*, October 22, 2000.

4. Teresa F. Lindeman, "Former Payless Chief Hits Pay Dirt with Build-A-Bear," *Pittsburgh Post-Gazette*, August 3, 2001

5. Clark, interview.

6. Ibid.

7. Ibid.

8. Ibid.

9. Ibid.

10. Ibid.

11. Ibid.

12. Ibid.

13. Ibid.

14. *www.theacsi.org*

15. Clark, interview.

16. Teresa Kroll, telephone interview with authors, 26 February, 2002.

17. Ibid.

18. Clark, interview.

19. Ibid.

20. Ibid.

21. Ibid.

22. Ibid.

23. Kroll, interview.

24. Mel Duvall, "Top 10 Companies to Work For," *Interactive Week*, April 9, 2001.

25. Kroll, interview.

26. Clark, interview.

27. Ibid.

28. Ibid.
29. Kroll, interview.
30. Ibid.
31. Ibid.
32. Ibid.
33. Clark, interview.

Chapter 13: Southwest Airlines: A Cause, Not Just an Airline

1. Kim Clark, "Nothing But the Plane Truth," *U.S. News & World Report,* 31 December 2001.

2. From a packet of letters the company provided to the authors.

3. Jim Parker, comments made during "Message to the Field" employee meeting in Chicago, Illinois, 25 March 2002.

4. Ibid.

5. "Air Herb's Secret Weapon," *Chief Executive,* 1999, *chiefexecutive .net/mag/146/article1.htm.*

6. "Flight Attendants Can Be Humorous, Too," *www.lovedungeon.net /humor/misc/attendants.html.*

7. *Chief Executive.*

8. Parker, comments.

9. Linda Rutherford, interview with authors, Dallas, Texas, 30 January 2002.

10. Kevin Krone, interview with authors, Dallas, Texas, 30 January 2002.

11. Parker, comments.

12. John Huey, "The Jack and Herb Show," *eCompany,* January 1999.

13. *Chief Executive.*

14. Herb Kelleher, "A Culture of Commitment," *Leader to Leader,* Spring 1997.

15. *www.iflyswa.com/help/luvbook.html*

16. Clark, "Nothing But the Plane Truth."

17. Rich Marcotte, telephone interview with authors, 7 March 2002.

18. Parker, comments.

19. Patty Kryscha, interview with authors, Chicago, Illinois 18 February 2002.

20. Ibid.

21. Ibid.

Chapter 14: IBM: The Billion-Dollar Cause

1. Robert McMillan, "Friendly, Big and Blue: In a world of upstarts, is IBM becoming Linux's father figure?" *Linux Magazine,* October 2000.

2. *www.linux10.org/history*

3. David Worthington, "IBM Backs Linux with $100 Million," *Beta-News,* 18 February 2005.

4. Joe Wilcox, "IBM to Spend $1 Billion on Linux in 2001," *News .com,* 12 December 2000.

5. Eric S. Raymond, *The Cathedral and the Bazaar.* (Sebastopol, California: O'Reilly, 2001).

6. Jeff "Hemos" Bates, e-mail interview with authors, various dates 25 March 2002–15 April 2002.

7. McMillan, "Friendly, Big and Blue."

8. Mary Jo Foley, "IBM's Palmisano touts Linux at confab," *News.com,* 31 January 2001.

9. Photo of "Peace. Love. Linux" street campaign by Rich Hein. Reprinted with special permission from the *Chicago Sun-Times.* Copyright 2002.

10. Tim O'Reilly, interviews with authors, 6 February–2 April 2002.

11. Spencer E. Ante, "Big Blue's Big Bet on Free Software," *Business Week,* 10 December 2001.

12. Bates, interview.

13. O'Reilly, interview.

14. *slashdot.org/articles/01/02/13/0254220.shtml*

15. *screaming-penguin.com*

16. *www.redmonk.com/sogrady/archives/001339.html*

17. Guy Kawasaki, interview with authors, 8 February 2002.

18. William J. Holstein, "Big Blue Wages Open Warfare," *Businesss 2.0,* April 2001.

19. Irving Wladawsky-Berger, speech to IBM Technical Developer Conference, San Francisco, August 2001. *www.ibm.com/news/us/2001/08/15.html*

20. McMillan, "Friendly, Big and Blue."

21. Wilcox, "IBM to spend $1 billion on Linux in 2001."

22. Ed Oswald, "IBM Pledges 500 Patents to Open Source," *Beta-News,* 22 January 2005.

23. Katie Dean, "IBM Expands Open Source," *TheStreet.com,* 15 August 2006.

24. Worthington, "IBM Backs Linux with $100 Million."

Cialdini, Robert B. *Influence: The Psychology of Persuasion.* Rev. ed. New York: William Morrow, 1993.

Cross, Richard, and Janet Smith. *Customer Bonding: 5 Steps to Lasting Customer Loyalty.* Lincolnwood, Illinois: NTC Business Books, 1995.

Dawkins, Richard. *The Selfish Gene.* Oxford: Oxford University Press, 1990.

Giovagnoli, Melissa and Jocelyn Carter-Miller. *Networlding: Building Relationships for Opportunities and Success.* San Francisco: Jossey-Bass, 2000.

Gladwell, Malcolm. *The Tipping Point: How Little Things Can Make a Big Difference.* Boston: Little, Brown and Company, 2000.

Godin, Seth. *Unleashing the Ideavirus.* Do You Zoom, Inc., 2000.

Godin, Seth. *Permission Marketing.* New York: Simon & Schuster, 1999.

Kawasaki, Guy. *Rules for Revolutionaries: The Capitalist Manifesto for Creating and Marketing New Products and Services.* HarperBusiness, 1999.

Kawasaki, Guy. *Selling the Dream: How to Promote Your Product, Company, or Ideas—and Make a Difference—Using Everyday Evangelism.* New York: HarperCollins, 1991.

Kotler, Philip. *Marketing Management: Analysis, Planning, Implementation & Control.* 10th ed. Englewood Cliffs, New Jersey: Prentice Hall, 1991.

Kotler, Philip, and Gary Armstrong. *Principles of Marketing.* 5th ed. Englewood Cliffs, New Jersey: Prentice Hall, 1991.

McClure, Evelyn S. *Sebastopol, California: History, Homes, and People, 1855–1920.* Belle View Press, 1995.

Pallotta, Dan. *When Your Moment Comes: A Guide to Fulfilling Your Dreams by a Man Who Has Led Thousands to Greatness.* San Diego, California: Jodere Group, 2001

Pine, Joseph, and James H. Gilmore. *The Experience Economy.* Boston: Harvard Business Review Press, 1999.

Pink, Daniel P. *Free Agent Nation: How America's New Independent Workers Are Transforming the Way We Live.* New York: Warner, 2001.

Porter, Michael E. *Competitive Strategy.* New York: Free Press, 1980.

Raymond, Eric S. *The Cathedral and the Bazaar.* Sebastopol, California: O'Reilly, 2001.

Reichheld, Frederick F. *The Loyalty Effect.* Boston: Harvard Business School Press, 1996.

Reichheld, Frederick F. *Loyalty Rules!* Boston: Harvard Business School Press, 2001

Rosen, Emanuel. *The Anatomy of Buzz: How to Create Word of Mouth Marketing.* New York: Currency Doubleday, 2000.

Sanders, Tim. *Love Is the Killer App.* New York: Crown Business, 2002.

Seybold, Patrica B., and Ronni T. Marshak. *Customers.com: How to Create a Profitable Business Strategy for the Internet and Beyond.* New York: Times Business, 1998.

Shenk, Jim. *Data Smog.* Harper San Francisco. 1998 (revised).

Siegel, David. *Futurize Your Enterprise: Business Strategy in the Age of the E-Customer.* New York: John Wiley & Sons, 1999.

Silverman, George. *Secrets of Word-of-Mouth Marketing: How to Trigger Exponential Sales through Runaway Word of Mouth.* New York: AMACOM, 2001.

L

Lightner, Candy, 87
Lindsey, Barbara, 43
Linux, 82, 185–94
Lord of the Rings movie Web site, 75
Love Is the Killer App (Sanders), 23
Loyalty, short *vs.* long-term, 25
Loyalty Effect, The (Reichheld), 23, 25
Lurker, The, 36–38

M

McCarthy, E. Jerome, 7
McCool, Rob, 51
McGee-Cooper, Ann, 1–2
McKinsey & Company, 54
McKinsey-Jupiter Media Metrix, 71
MacWorld, 58
Maker's Mark Ambassadors, 72
Marcotte, Rich, 180–82
Margulies, Anne, 52–53
Mark Cuban Show, The, 142
Marketing
  see also Customer evangelism
  advertising as, 7–8
  budgets, 8
  cause-related, 88–90
  current problems in, 5–10
  desperation and, 9
  e-mail, 203–5
  glamorization in media of, 8
  grassroots marketing, 104
  humanization of, 75–76
  recessions and, 4
Massachusetts Institute of Technology, 51
Mass advertising, 8
May Department Stores Company, 98, 154–55
Mayer, Brown, Rowe & Maw, 54
Media relations, 108–10
Meme, 68
Microsoft, 21, 75, 93–94, 122–23, 186–87, 189
MicroSolutions, 138, 139
MIT Open CourseWare, 52–53
Momentum Marketing, 106
Montgomery Ward, 153
Mothers Against Drunk Driving (MADD), 87
Mrak, Val, 111
Museum of Contemporary Art, 111

N

Napster, 47–48, 139
Napsterized industries, 51–54
Napsterizing knowledge, 13, 47–54, 198, 209
National Audubon Society, 93, 95
National Quality Research Center, 159

National Rifle Association (NRA), 92, 95
National Underwriter, 48
Nelson, Don, 142
Nestlé USA, 39–40
New Line Cinema, 65
Newsletters, e-mail, 74
Newsweek Japan, 110
NeXT, 92
Nowitzki, Dirk, 147

O

Ogilvy, David, 9
Olsen, Kevin, 107
One Smooth Stone, 107
Online
  bulletin boards, 74–75, 199–200, 212
  surveys, 41–43
Open source. *See* IBM/Linux connection
Opt-in e-mail list, 212
Oracle, 51
Oral B, 91
O'Reilly, Christina, 124
O'Reilly, Tim, 3, 50, 119–33, 191
O'Reilly Media, 74, 119–33
  availability of company knowledge, 129–32
  conventions and conferences, 129
  customer communities and, 126–28
  customer feedback and, 130–33
  evangelism scorecard, 132–33
  marketing strategy of, 121–24
  product line, 126–27
Orwell, George, 86

P

Paddison, Gordon, 65
Paddock, Simone, 128
PAETEC, 13
Pallotta, Dan, 91–92
Pallotta TeamWorks, 91
Palmisano, Sam, 189
Parker, Jim, 172–73, 176–78, 182
Patel, Marilyn Hall, 47–48
Payless Shoe Source, 154
Pepsi, 24
perl.com, 129
Permission Marketing (Godin), 25
Perot, Ross Jr., 139
Petersen, Randy, 39
Phone companies, 24
Pickering, Charles F. Sr., 97
Pine, Joseph, 63
Pink, Dan, 105–7
Pitch, 206–8
Planned Parenthood, 93, 96–97
Pocket Innovator (KnowBrainer), 100, 102–3
Popcorn, Faith, 83

PotterWar, 75
PowerBar, 58
Procter & Gamble, 43, 62, 81
Product(s)
  greatness of, 20
  samples, 200
  trial, 80
Professional services industry, 54
Prokos, George, 144, 151
Promotion, 7, 25
Promotion Marketing Association, 81
Public relations, buzz and, 58–59
Publishing industry, 53

R

Raymond, Eric S., 188
Recording Industry Association of America, 47
Reichheld, Fred, 6, 25
Retail industry, 154–57. *See also* Build-A-Bear Workshop
Retail Innovator of the Year award, 155
Ring, Benjamin, 114
Roehm, Julie, 62
Rosen, Emanuel, 55–56, 105
Rutherford, Linda, 177

S

Safari online book program, 130, 132
Samples, trial, 80
Samuels, Bill Jr., 72–73
Samuels, Bill Sr., 72
Sanders, Tim, 23, 65
Sanders, William, 37–38
Scott, Ridley, 86
Scriba, Paul, 34–35
SEAMS model, 20
Sears, 153
Sebastopol, California, 119–20, 124
Secrets of Word–of–Mouth Advertising (Silverman), 20
Securitization.net, 54
Selfish Gene, The (Dawkins), 68
Selling the Dream (Kawasaki), 92
Selvin, Joel, 49
September 11 terrorist attacks, 171
Service, greatness of, 20
Shareholder value, 17–18
Shenk, David, 8
Shouldice, Edward Earle, 69
Shouldice Hospital, 69–71
Sierra Club, 91, 97–98, 126
Silverman, George, 20
Siteman Cancer Center, 164
slashdot.org, 189
Sloane Communications, 34–35
Smith, Janet, 88
Software industry, 51